THE SHORES OF PENRHYN LLŶN

The Llyn Peninsula

THE SHORES OF PENRHYN LLŶN

The Llyn Peninsula

by Maurice Hope

DB PUBLISHING

First published in Great Britain in 2007 by
The Breedon Books Publishing Company Limited
Breedon House, 3 The Parker Centre, Derby, DE21 4SZ.

This paperback edition published in Great Britain in
2014 by DB Publishing, an imprint of JMD Media Ltd

Dedication

In 2003 my wife and I came to live in a small village in Eifionydd.
We were warmly welcomed by our new neighbours.
This book is dedicated to them.

ISBN 978-1-78091-443-5

Printed and bound in the UK by Copytech (UK) Ltd
Peterborough

Contents

	Acknowledgements	7
	Introduction	9
Part I	Eifionydd	
I	Tremadog	12
	Madog's Cob	19
II	Porthmadog	22
	Enter Mr Holland	26
III	Y Garth	34
	Promenade: Porthmadog to Borth-y-Gest	37
IV	Borth-y-Gest	38
	Promenade: Borth-y-Gest to Cricieth	40
V	Cricieth	42
	Promenade: Cricieth to Llanystumdwy	51
VI	Lloyd George's village	53
	One Life	58
	Promenade: Llanystumdwy to Pwllheli	59
Part II	Llŷn and Arfon	
VII	Pwllheli	63
	The Labours of Solomon	69
	Promenade: West End to Llanbedrog	74
VIII	Plas Glyn-y-Weddw, The Widow's Glen	77
	Promenade: Llanbedrog to Abersoch	82
IX	Abersoch	85
	A Family Album	95
	Dear Motorist	101
	The Proverbial Slate	102
X	Plas yn Rhiw	104
	Hell's Mouth and *The Twelve Apostles*	107
	Around Rhiw	108
	Promenade: Rhiw to Aberdaron	110
XI	Aberdaron	111
	Richard Robert Jones	114
	Promenade: Aberdaron to Mynydd Mawr	115
XII	Llanllawen to Porth Dinllaen	118
	An Entertaining and Instructive Visit to Tudweiliog	123
XIII	Porth Dinllaen	125
	Promenade: Porth Dinllaen to Nefyn	129

XIV	Nefyn	130
	Pilgrims' Retreat	134
	Promenade: St Beuno's to Nant Gwrtheyrn	135
XV	Nant Gwrtheyrn (Vortigern's Valley)	136
	Vortigern	140
	The Curses	141
	The *Amy Summerfield* story	143
	Promenade: Nant Gwrtheyrn to Trefor	144
XVI	Trefor	146
	Promenade: Trefor to Clynnog Fawr	148
	Clynnog Fawr	150
XVII	Pontllyfni Beach	153
XVIII	Lords and Ladies	159
	Glynllifon	164
	Maria Stella	168
	Promenade: Llandwrog to Caernarfon	172
	Notes	178
	Glossary of Place Names	180
	References	182
	Other Sources	183

Acknowledgements

I am most grateful to Tony and Gwenllian Jones at rhiw.com, for allowing me to use images from their extensive archive and for their advice regarding sources and copyright; to historian and writer Gwilym Jones, for making available his personal collection of photographs and documents, for his contribution to the text and for his unstinting encouragement; to author Tom Morris, whose books about Porth Dinllaen and Morfa Nefyn represent a unique resource; to Miriam Grant, Information Co-ordinator at the Welsh Language and Heritage Centre, Nant Gwrtheyrn, who read my drafts, checked my use of Welsh names and phrases, and provided much support; and to the late Gwyn Ellis, for allowing me to use his Porth Nant photographs.

I would like to thank Jan Morris, for allowing me to include references to her life and work.

I am indebted to my neighbours Henry and Anne Roberts, who somehow managed to locate a gold mine of old photographs and documents, and who also contributed to the text; to John Jones, who has made computer skills into an art form; to the numerous people who provided me with original images – Peter Leslie, Oliver Hodgson, David Clement, Jim Mowat, Michael Leeks and Catriona and Rodney Bracewell (including some fine aerial views); and to all those who have lent or given miscellaneous items – prints, books, maps etc – Ann Jones, 'Bonzo' Jones, Sheila Selfe, Sharron Jones, Madeleine Downie, Gwynfor and Dorothy Hughes, the Revd Michael Walker, Eunice Jones and Gwynedd Roberts, the manager of Glynllifon.

I would also like to thank Bear Print of Porthmadog, for a degree of patience equalled only by Lynda Purnell, my long-suffering typist.

Finally, I must thank Cath, my daughter, for her lively, evocative drawings and my wife Margaret, for her professional insights and unwavering support.

The Llyn Peninsula

1. Tremadog
2. Porthmadog
3. Y Garth
4. Borth-y-gest
5. Cricieth
6. Llanystumdwy
7. Pwllheli
8. Llanbedrog
9. Abersoch
10. Rhiw
11. Aberdaron
12. Llanllawen
13. Porth Dinllaen
14. Nefyn
15. Nant Gwrtheyrn
16. Trefor
17. Pontllyfni
18. Llandwrog

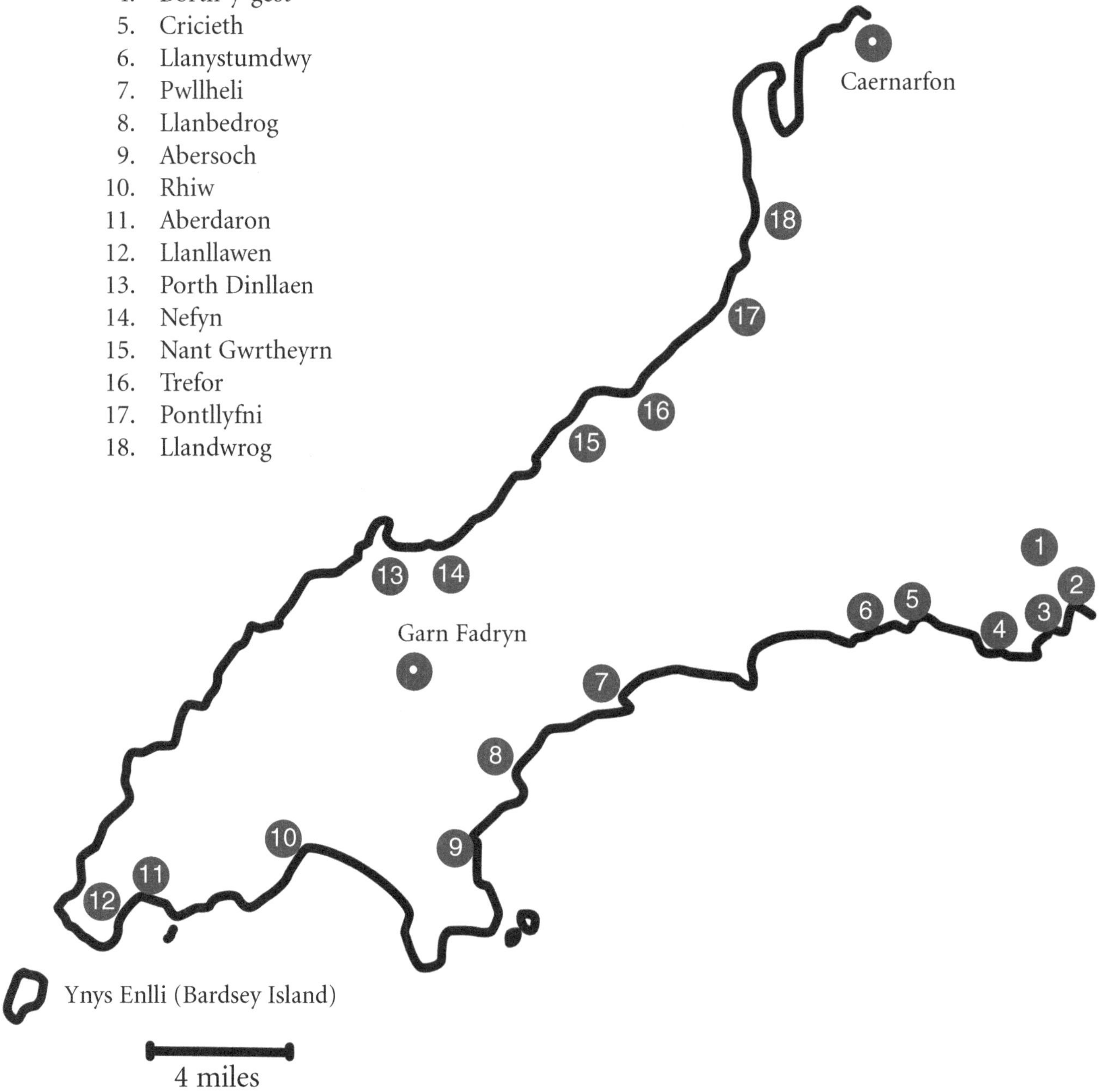

INTRODUCTION

Glance at a map of North Wales and you will notice a tapering finger of land, somewhat less than 30 miles long, pointing across the sea to Ireland. This is Penrhyn Llŷn, the Llyn Peninsula: hills and headlands spilling into the surrounding waters, appearing almost as an aftershock to the great mountains of Eryri (Snowdonia), which dramatically furnish her landward horizon. At the Peninsula's eastern end – 15 miles apart, an imaginary line between them creating a rather arbitrary boundary – stand the Madogs and Caernarfon. The 'new' and the old. Gateways or sentinels, as you choose. Our journey will take us from the one, around the shores of Penrhyn Llŷn, towards the other.

Although the mountains here cannot compete with the rugged peaks of Eryri, the Peninsula can boast many a dramatic height from which it is possible to observe her scale and form: Tre'r Ceiri, the Town of Giants, for example, Moel-y-Gest towering over the Madogs, or Garn Fadryn, an isolated Iron Age hill fort midway between Tudweiliog and Llanbedrog.

The view from Garn Fadryn is all-embracing: in the foreground, scattered remains of ancient dwellings and fortifications; below, in every direction, Penrhyn Llŷn spreading out around you. Beyond the Peninsula, a sweeping panorama from Eryri to the seaboard and mountains of Ceredigion, and as far as the distant tongues – or rather, Heads – of Strumble and St David's: in the north, Ynys Môn (Anglesey); to the west, the Wicklow Hills.

Garn Fadryn. rhiw.com

Garn Fadryn in spring.

rhiw.com

But now look again to the Llŷn with her swirls and checks of greens, greys and ochres; fields, woods, heath; patchworks of heather and gorse; crags, screes and standing stones. Observe her scattered boulders and shadowy uplands; her stone farmsteads, lime-washed cottages and pebble-dashed terraces; country lanes – seen then unseen – climbing, falling, wandering carelessly from farm to village to harbour; churches with stocky towers and slender bellcotes; monolithic chapels; streams and rivers slipping into a slate-blue sea; the sun catching the water, kindling distant pools of white light.

To the east, the Madogs, Cricieth (Criccieth)[1] and Pwllheli, the headland of Llanbedrog and the gently-curving beaches of Abersoch. Farther south, Mynydd Cilan, Rhiw and, between them, the mouth of Hell – Porth Neigwl. Beyond Hell – south-west of Aberdaron and Mynydd Mawr – Ynys Enlli (Bardsey Island), the island in the currents, holiest of holies and, in days gone by, sanctuary for countless pilgrims.

Hell and heaven face to face! Hell, smiling her pleasant moon-smile and lapped, apparently, by gentle waters, while being in reality precisely-shaped for disaster; heaven – or so it would seem – brooding, forbidding. Where did you ever see a more menacing God or a more benign Devil?

Turn north now, past a succession of craggy coves – Porth Oer, Penllech, Ychain, Ysgaden, names unruly to the outsider's eye and tongue – to Porth Dinllaen, the Nefyns, Nant Gwrtheyrn, Yr Eifl – the so-called Rivals – plunging inexorably into the sea and, secreted behind them, Trefor, Clynnog Fawr and Caernarfon.

So much, and much more you can see. But what you cannot detect from your Iron Age fortress are Penrhyn Llŷn's energies and passions. You cannot sense her pride, her engagement with tradition, her hospitality. You cannot tell that music, art and poetry flourish here, or that Cymraeg – the ancient language of the Welsh – inhabits every street.[2]

PART I: EIFIONYDD

I TREMADOG

Look now north-east towards the humps of Moel-y-Gest and the Madogs – Tremadog and Porthmadog. Madog's town and Madog's port. Here in the town, our journey begins.

Even today, given the wildness of its situation, Tremadog – spacious, formal, a little 'unreal' – takes you by surprise. In its infancy, during the early years of the 19th century, not only must it have seemed a fantastic apparition to the local populace, but it must also have astonished even the most seasoned traveller.

Think of it. It is 1810 or thereabouts, and while in the surrounding areas life has shuffled on in its usual, unhurried way, a new town – or 'borough', as its founder would have it – has appeared on the salt marshes at the western edge of Traeth Mawr, the Great Beach. Rumours about this amazing place have excited curiosity, and people have come from miles around to see it for themselves.

The once-waterlogged approaches are firm. The roads are good. An embankment has secured and drained what must be nearly 2,000 acres of marshland. An orderly terrace of stone cottages stands beside a large factory – a textile mill – noisy with activity. A graceful two-storey building with elegant arches and tall windows stands tight against the steep face of rock. There is music and laughter, and behind the windows, figures flit by – ladies and gentlemen dancing. There is a proscenium arch, a gallery and a small orchestra.

In front of the building there is an open square – a market place –

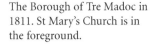

The Borough of Tre Madoc in 1811. St Mary's Church is in the foreground.

The former Town Hall and Dancing Room, Market Square.
Peter Leslie

and people are strolling and chattering, many of them in languages unfamiliar to local ears. Shops, inns and cottages fit neatly around three sides of the square, and, a little way along the road towards the shore, half-a-dozen workers are putting the finishing touches to a sober-looking chapel.

It is like a foreign country, a fable or fantasy. Strange tongues and exotic buildings; pillars and arches set before walls of rock; bespoke trees posing in expanses of gorse and scrub; streets called Dublin and London; and – impossibly romantic – glimpses of ships' masts in the very heart of town.

There will be more. A Gothic church will rise from a small island beside the road, a tramway will run along the canal bank and a clutter of railways – Croesor, Porthmadog, Cambrian – will create such confusion as to make the mind spin. Shelley will walk these streets, Elizabeth Billington will perform arias here and in 1888, T. E. Lawrence, 'Lawrence of Arabia', will be born in this very borough.

Yet notwithstanding the area's isolation, travellers bound for the Irish Sea had passed this way for many decades. They would brave the

Opposite: The birthplace of Lawrence of Arabia, now known as Snowdon Lodge.

difficult journey through the harsh interior of Wales, defy the treacherous marshes of the Traeth and head west across the Peninsula to the small harbour of Porth Dinllaen.

Stimulated by the Act of Union with Ireland, such journeys had dramatically increased during the early years of the 19th century, and it had been largely to take advantage of the commercial opportunities thereby created that Tre Madoc had been established.

The borough's founder was William Alexander Madocks, who – though Welsh of ancestry – was born in London in 1773. Fascinated by the wild beauty of the land of his forefathers, he would often travel to North Wales, however disagreeable the journey.

Known as an Irredeemable Romantic, Mr Madocks's idealism was nevertheless moderated by a shrewd, entrepreneurial eye, and it was this quality which enabled him to visualise the potential benefits of developing these desolate lands. Tre Madoc would be a staging post on the route to Ireland and as such would represent a tangible element of that vision.

Yet there was much to do: land to be remodelled, sea to be subdued, roads to be cut and a borough to be founded and activated! It would be, however, a great adventure; one undertaken in a spirit of undiluted optimism, in which successes would be assumed and setbacks drowned 'in drafts of brisk champagne'.

Though Mr Madocks himself – Member of Parliament for Boston in Lincolnshire – would often be busy elsewhere, he could take heart from the efforts of his local manager, John Williams, for he knew that Mr Williams shared his dream. And on the occasions when Madocks returned to Wales, he would survey the work in progress from 'Tan yr Allt', his splendid villa high above the Great Beach – a villa 'fit for an Indian Prince' – and would no doubt plan even more ambitious schemes for the future.

Madocks looks down upon his creation.

The old coaching inn now called The Royal Madoc Arms Hotel.

Like many a romantic, William Madocks had a heightened awareness of the world around him. He knew that this was by no means the first occasion that Tracth Mawr and its environs had figured in the journals of history. Indeed, in 1170 a momentous event had occurred close to this very spot. For it was from here that a certain Prince Madog set sail across the western seas, a voyage which would conclude, gloriously, with the discovery of America! Now, although William Madocks could claim no fundamental link with his royal near-namesake, he was perhaps gratified by their nominal similarity and inspired by the prince's great enterprise. It was not unreasonable, therefore, for him to cultivate the romantic resonance of the coincidence, and to shrewdly adopt the august name for his town and his port.

As for the weary traveller who came upon Tre Madoc, what unanticipated pleasures awaited him: an evening ball and eisteddfod, a hilarious performance of Mr Sheridan's *The Rivals*, an afternoon at the races. How could he possibly have predicted that a business trip, regarded no doubt, as a tedious obligation, would become in fact an experience to live in his memory.

St Mary's Church. The final stages of restoration, August 2006.

The Coadstone gateway of St Mary's. It was shipped in sections to Tre Madoc from London.

The home of conservationist Cecily Edith Williams-Ellis MBE, from 1958 to 1991.

And there was more. For when the traveller finally reached Porth Dinllaen, he would have done so in the belief that he himself had played a small part in the making of history: for the road he had followed would one day become the major route to the coast, and Porth Dinllaen would be adopted as the primary gateway to Ireland. Or so it appeared.

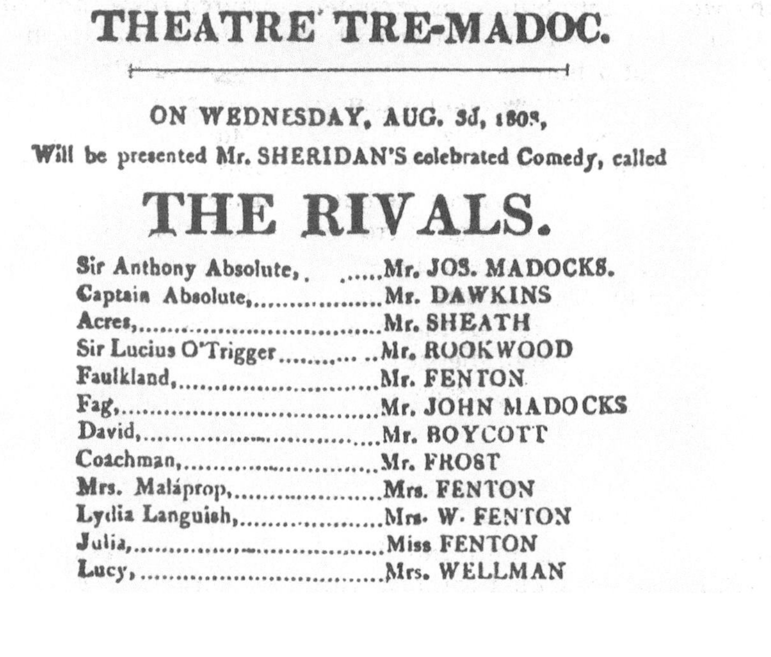

THEATRE TRE-MADOC.

ON WEDNESDAY, AUG. 3d, 1808,

Will be presented Mr. SHERIDAN'S celebrated Comedy, called

THE RIVALS.

Sir Anthony Absolute, ...Mr. JOS. MADOCKS.
Captain Absolute,..................Mr. DAWKINS
Acres,..................................Mr. SHEATH
Sir Lucius O'Trigger.......... ..Mr. ROOKWOOD
Faulkland,............................Mr. FENTON
Fag,.....................................Mr. JOHN MADOCKS
David,..................................Mr. BOYCOTT
Coachman,...........................Mr. FROST
Mrs. Malàprop,......................Mrs. FENTON
Lydia Languish,.....................Mrs. W. FENTON
Julia,....................................Miss FENTON
Lucy,....................................Mrs. WELLMAN

An evening with Mr Sheridan.

MADOG'S COB

Notwithstanding the glories of Tre Madoc, Mr Madocks's restless aspirations were unfulfilled, and, though he may have been thought quite mad, he set off to survey the vast and inhospitable wasteland of Traeth Mawr itself. He dreamed of creating fruitful lands there, and even – with the building of roads and railways – of revolutionising communications with deepest Wales.

The conquest of the Traeth would be far from easy to execute. It would require huge resources, not only of will and determination but also of finance. Thousands of acres of marshland to be drained, the Afon Glaslyn to be diverted and a massive embankment, a mile in length, to be built! Yet Mr Madocks firmly resolved 'to give birth, shape and substance' to this most audacious plan, and he obtained, in due course, appropriate parliamentary consent. Once again, John Williams was appointed to manage the deed, while Madocks himself – often from afar – conjured with all measures financial, diplomatic and visionary.

Once underway, the project became a nerve-tingling cycle of construction and destruction. Working sites were frequently inundated by tide-driven torrents of sand, the work of several months sometimes being destroyed in a few hours. In a desperate search for secure foundations engineers would reach depths of 80 feet. And while John Williams and his men toiled and endured, Madocks would instruct, exhort and assail his stricken manager with a ceaseless barrage of letters, sketches and schedules.

Inch by inch, however, the arms of the embankment converged, and finally – though it took more than three years – the gap between them was sealed. Treath Mawr was at last imprisoned. In September 1811 a great celebration was arranged. There would be dancing, singing and horse racing. An ox would be roasted, harpists would play and poets declaim. Mr Madocks was exultant. 'All the world shall attend our Jubilee,' he wrote.

Long after the celebrations are done, visitors continue to flock to this object of wonder – Madocks's Cob. For a small fee they can stroll across it from county to county, feel on their cheeks the westerlies that had so recently represented the enemy of progress, contemplate newly-facilitated sea views and – to the east – uncustomary mountain scapes. And although this chunky, unrefined and quite unbeautiful causeway may not represent a feast to the architectural gourmet, or a gift to the aesthete, it is nevertheless auspicious. It is both elemental and functional, and it would be churlish to think badly of it.

But soon, inevitably, questions arise. How might the redeemed land best be utilised? How might the embankment be made even more secure? How – since the Afon Glaslyn has been unsettled by its rude diversion – might the river's access to the sea be better managed? Would

'All the world shall attend our Jubilee.'

Trè-Madoc Embankment Jubilee.

An OX will be roafted upon the Middle of the Embankment

at 12 o'Clock on TUESDAY the 17th of SEPTEMBER, 1811.

The RACES will follow, and continue the 18th and 19th.

An EISTEDDFOD will likewife be held, when a Silver Cup will be given to the beft Welch Poet, and another to the beft Welch Harper.

There will be an Ordinary at the two Inns at four o'Clock on Monday the 16th, and the three following Days.

Alfo Plays, Balls, &c. in the Evening.

a lock gate be feasible? And – not least – how might impatient creditors be distracted and new monies located?

It is winter 1812, and violent gales and prodigious tides pound the embankment. Time and again they rush forward, probing for weaknesses. In February – even before the highest tides of the season – the waters burst through, race across Traeth Mawr, and threaten the Cob with total destruction.

As shock and frustration subside, however, and restoration begins, a miraculous sense of brotherhood emerges from local communities. Subscriptions pour in and an army of workers appears as if by magic. According to a contemporary account, at one point the workforce comprises no fewer than 892 men and 737 horses! (Although at another time, it should be said, John Williams's labourers – pushed too hard, unpaid and close to starvation – unceremoniously troop from the site.)

Yet soon, financial resources are stretched again. They cannot possibly match demand. Mr Madocks, plagued by gout as well as by debt, remains ensconced in England, his scheme, if not his hopes, increasingly close to collapse. But however urgent the crisis, he pushes on, speaking enthusiastically about employing expensive modern techniques to cultivate his reclaimed lands, about laying a road to Harlech, and even railway lines to Ffestiniog and Trawsfynydd. Nothing, it seems, can deter him.

In what must surely constitute the most bizarre of events, Percy Bysshe Shelley – who has temporarily rented 'Tan yr Allt' and who regards Mr Madocks as a revolutionary soul mate – lends passionate support to the great adventure. He addresses meetings and undertakes fund-raising activities. For a time the involvement of such a celebrity is

A BILL

To amend two Acts of His late and present Majesty's Reign, for vesting the sands of Traeth Mawr, in the Counties of Carnarvon and Merioneth, in William Alexander Madocks Esquire, and for building Quays and other Works at the Harbour of Port Madoc, in the said County of Carnarvon.

The opening statement of the Port Madoc Harbour Bill of 1826

uplifting, but in due course – as befits a Romantic poet – Shelley courts controversy, is implicated in a firearms incident, and flees to Ireland.

The wheel spins once more, and by dint of prodigious effort and improving fortunes the embankment is finally restored. Madocks's brother, Joseph, provides an unexpected financial lifeline, the Government fortuitously declares a shortage of new lands for cultivation, and even Nature herself – she who has striven so hard to thwart Mr Madocks's ambitions – decides, though not quite yet, to reward his undying tenacity with an improbable prize.

Elegant Kerfoot's.

Cath Hope

II Porthmadog

A birds-eye view of Porthmadog (formerly Portmadoc) shows a web of closely-woven streets, a trio of railways, and a meeting of roads from Ffestiniog, Pwllheli, Beddgelert and Caernarfon. It is a hub and an inescapable bottleneck. A by-pass is constantly discussed.

Approaching the town from the Tremadog direction – passing the Welsh Highland Railway on your left – you will immediately enter Stryd Fawr (High Street): leisure centre, supermarket, little offshoots of terraced houses, cinema, The Royal Sportsman Hotel, and – to the right – Kerfoot's, an elegant department store 'Where shopping is a Sheer Delight,' and has been since 1874. Kerfoot's, of the gracious, symmetrical timbered façade, the beautiful spiral staircase and millennium stained-glass dome. Seeing this fine old shop gazing out over the hubbub, reflecting perhaps upon a less frenetic age, you might well wonder if she does so with a tinge of regret.

Here, at the small roundabout, you have reached the neck of the bottle, and for the next half mile or so progress will be restricted. But

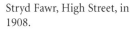

Stryd Fawr, High Street, in 1908.

don't be discouraged, for your predicament will allow you to observe Stryd Fawr in all its glory: pavements dense with humankind of every shape and size, standing about, shuffling along, window-gazing, feeding, colliding with pushchairs or with the fishing nets and sparkly windmills that now and then spill out before you; serious shoppers, baskets bulging, neat professionals darting through the mêlée, farmers in civvies, elderly couples in summer beige.

St John's Church.

And look at the street's goodly array of shops, galleries, cafés and inns. See how her buildings divide: at street level, cheerful, on-the-go, strictly 21st century; upper storeys, more diffident, their fretwork and added stucco mementoes of days gone by. Notice, too, the occasional once-splendid villa, protruding uncomfortably from the ranks of unfeeling shop fronts, and observe her

The Royal Sportsman Hotel.

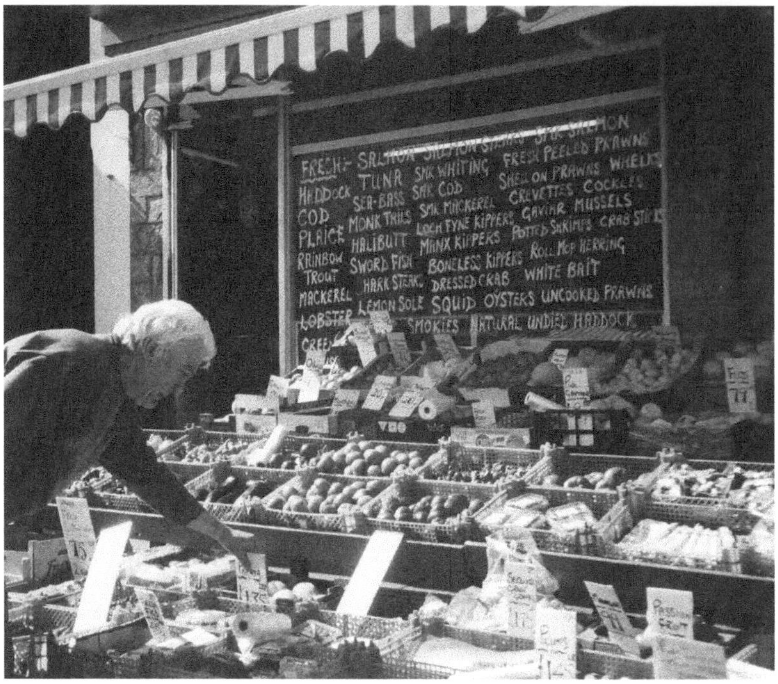

Joe Lewis's groaning table of delights.

imposing banks and mirthless chapels – houses of Mammon, houses of God – locked seemingly, in some architectural (not to say spiritual) competition. Glimpse the fearsome church of Bank Place – Eglwys Presbyteraidd Cymru Y Garth (its name as daunting as its demeanour) – or Salem, the poker-faced chapel standing back, distancing itself from the crowd. Salem, commending no doubt the respectable bookshop next door, but deprecating the ungodly sensuality of Joe Lewis's

The working harbour, the 'heartbeat of Portmadoc'.
Jim Mowat

bountiful emporium across the street – a groaning table of butternut squash, fresh horseradish, ginger, sweet potatoes; scotch bonnets, Nashi pears, and limes; cooked chestnuts and kumquats; oysters, squid, caviar; capons, pheasants, mallards and partridges; cheeses, wines. Joe Lewis, deadly sins incarnate!

On or near Stryd Fawr you can eat, drink and pray. You can buy a magnificent grand piano, a sheep-shy sheepdog, a landscape from Rob Piercy's gallery, a wedding band of Welsh gold, or a long-deleted vinyl disc from Cob, an extraordinary record shop. You can dance the salsa, sing with Abba and ride a steam train.

Yet for all that, Stryd Fawr is like many a high street in many a town. Except that Moel-y-Gest, Cnicht and Moelwyn Mawr peep at you from the side streets.

As you approach the lower end of the street – Llŷn Bach to your left, Madocks's Cob and the Ffestiniog Railway before you – you will see to your right Porthmadog Harbour. It lies low in a manner almost self-effacing, betraying little of its erstwhile importance. Its business now is mostly leisure, yet in the 19th century it was the heartbeat of Portmadoc[3], not so much enhancing the town's status as initiating it.

The origins of Portmadoc Harbour, unlike those of the region's other great enterprises, are largely accidental: a twist of fortune, a gift of nature few could have anticipated. For when Mr Madocks's embankment enclosed Traeth Mawr, it also restricted the Afon Glaslyn's

Dorothy, the first of the beautiful 'Western Ocean Yachts'.

access to the sea. Twice daily, as the tide rose, the river – made captive – was forced back upon itself; and twice daily, as the tide receded, river waters surged into the estuary, their force and turbulence delving into the bed below. A deep basin was scooped out from the mud. It was this basin which evolved into Portmadoc Harbour, and it was the harbour which awarded name, prosperity and celebrity to Madocks's port.

And – even more fateful – it befell that the building of a substantial harbour became feasible at the precise moment in history when reasons for its existence became compelling; that the revolutionary circumstances surrounding steam and slate, and the society they were beginning to forge, created the exact context for its good fortune; and, not least, that at the very moment in Madocks's life when he could most have benefitted from the inspiration afforded by a kindred spirit, such a person stepped out of the mist.

Enter Mr Holland

What enables history to do this? To provide, so often, the perfect convergence of circumstance and person? Is it providence? Alchemy? Divine calculation? Whatever it is, in 1821 a certain Samuel Holland tapped upon the Great Improver's door ready to do business.

These are the days of change and of opportunity: steam power flinging wide the gates of industry, factories sucking labour from the fields, towns crawling over virgin landscapes, and – across the world – a billion roofs to be hammered and slated. Samuel Holland is barely 20 years of age. He has been newly appointed to manage his father's slate company in Blaenau Ffestiniog, several miles east of Portmadoc. He is a man of action, unimpressed by the feebleness of caution.

In the uplands around Ffestiniog, quarrying is already well established. Over many years strong men have carved out a livelihood, and now, though slate companies share a degree of prosperity, many of their practices inevitably hark back to a slower world. The transportation of slate from quarry to sea for instance – involving a journey of several miles, not to mention a descent of 700 feet – is both clumsy and time consuming.

Imagine the assignment. Heavily-laden donkeys slither down muddy tracks to a road beside the Afon Dwyryd. At an approved place, slate is transferred to horse-drawn carts and is hauled downstream to the stone quays at tide's reach. Here, felt-hatted bargees – known as Philistines – transfer the cargo to flat-bottomed boats and head off across the bay to Ynys Cyngar, at the confluence of Glaslyn and Dwyryd, where the sea-going ships – small and cumbersome – are moored. It is tiresome, heavy work, so much effort for so meagre a load. But it bears the obligation of tradition, and no part of it is to be surrendered. It is a terrible task, but it is a tried and tested one. And it will not be compromised... not even if a new harbour were to attract slate-carrying vessels of four times the present capacity; not if it could claim the most up-to-date facilities for loading and repair; not even if a tramway were to descend from Ffestiniog to the harbour wharves themselves. Bold words!

Yet history is as much about breaking resolutions as about making them. So when Samuel Holland tapped upon Mr Madocks's door, pronounced his enthusiasm for the harbour enterprise, asked that a wharf be built in his name and even acknowledged the expediency of a

The brigantine *Edward Windus*, one of Portmadoc's famous phosphate carriers.

The splendid Town Hall, which once dominated the High Street, was demolished in the 1960s having been declared unsafe. Woolworth's now stands on the spot.

tramway from Ffestiniog – when he did these things, not only did his actions corroborate progress, not only did they signify a breaking of ranks, but they also planted the seeds to undermine the resolutions of the quarrymen and Philistines of Ffestiniog and the Dwyryd.

But at first they bide their time. They observe the construction of Mr Holland's wharf on Ynys Tywyn and await its effects. Then, when his increasing commercial advantages begin to register, they act. It is, they admit, a good harbour with excellent capacity. They seek wharves, at first casually, then urgently. They study locations. They sign contracts. John Williams, Madocks's enduring manager, is inundated, while Madocks himself is elated.

As the enterprise gains credibility, a few villas begin to appear at Ynys Tywyn, the hill behind the harbour, and the name Portmadoc slips into being. And as this occurs, people come to Portmadoc in increasing numbers.

The Ship, Portmadoc's oldest inn.

For while 'Madocks had laid the foundation for the future, Holland was building the edifice... (it was he who) beckoned people to come, and he did not call in vain... they came with their families, goods and chattels, and marched behind the... banner of young Holland.'[4]

Thus began the halcyon days. Ninety years – with the exception of the dismal 1870s – of dazzling progress. Portmadoc, bursting with confidence and ambition. Holland, pressing on, resolute and inventive: the Mutual Insurance Company, the tramway to Ffestiniog. Madocks had fortuitously discovered the executor of his dreams.

Pencei (Cornhill): at the head of the harbour, noisy with conviction, abuzz with the tactical and political wheeling of mariners and merchants; quaysides affluent and cosmopolitan with agents from the Baltic and Italy. Phosphate carriers from beyond 'the milky way'. Brigs and schooners swaggering and jostling. Wharves – mountainous with slate, timber, fish, spices – in such demand that a huge eminence of rock, Clogwyn-y-Pig, is torn down to facilitate expansion; an island of ballast rising from the water; brass and iron foundries, flourmills, a navigation college. Two, then four, then seven shipyards – order books overwhelmed; distinguished shipwrights – Ebenezer Roberts, David Jones, David Williams – rivalling and soon outflanking the builders of Pwllheli, creating nothing less than sea-going legends. The Western Ocean yachts, models of perfection, ruling the waves. And, across the world – in Casablanca, Cuba, Montevideo, Santa Fe – the name Portmadoc spoken in wonder.

The town, too, active in every way, keeping abreast of the port and able to boast, in 1886, 25 grocery stores, 18 inns, 14 slate merchants, nine butchers and nine cobblers, eight drapers, seven tailors, six insurance offices, five greengrocers and house furnishers, four superb hotels, coal merchants, surgeons and newsagents, four confectioners, three hairdressers, two printers and sparmakers, not to mention one bill poster.

In ancient times, you may recall, Prince Madog had set sail 'To

The Blodwen, the 'flower of the flock' of Western Ocean Yachts. She 'stood up to fresh breeze with the firmness of a rock'. In 1901, having loaded a full cargo of fish from Labrador, the *Blodwen* ran to Patras in Greece, a distance of 4,500 miles, in 22 days - over 200 miles a day.

Henry Hughes, 'Immortal Sails'.

discover rich lands in the east, but now a thousand sailed forth to distant shores in search of fortunes, and returned with the lockers of their little ships filled with gold and good things... They found the world had placed Portmadoc on the map.' (Henry Hughes)

Although the demand for slate diminishes in the first decade of the 20th century, it is World War One that effectively turns the tide. True, in the days thereafter, Portmadoc survives more than adequately, but she does not really prosper again until the onset of tourism... a poor substitute, many might say, for thriving industries, proud ships, great adventures and international esteem.

Today, as the 21st century gathers pace, the harbour remains the most evocative part of Porthmadog. It has been sensitively restored and, although the great ships have passed into antiquity and the engines of maritime supremacy have vanished, it is a place that might yet rouse the imagination. Slate, clean and smooth, remains its currency. Not in stacks and ranks awaiting shipment, but in pavements, walls, quays, sills and benches.

To reach the harbour on foot, turn right off Stryd Fawr at the Canolfan (Community Centre) and cross Y Clwt, where, even before the quays were made, ships would have been built. Samuel Holland's wharf is on the left, just across the channel. Stroll along Greaves Wharf towards the one remaining slate shed, a building now shared between Harbourmaster and Maritime Museum. Call in at the museum and speak, if you will, to the custodian. But do allow yourself plenty of time, for he will regale you with many a tale of courage and of hardship. Before your very eyes he will rebuild a coastal slate trader, and resurrect the spirits of long-departed captains and rugged pilots. He will lament the losses of *Annie Lloyd* and the *Sedulous*, and acclaim the derring-do of the port's gallant steam tugs.

But he will reserve the most lyrical poetry for the Newfoundland Clippers of 1889–1913 – the Great Western Ocean yachts. The *Blodwen* for example, built by David Jones not very far from the museum door. How frail she had looked on her stocks. Especially for one of whom so much would be required. Under 200 tons, and yet she would be expected to negotiate the mightiest storms and most stupendous seas. Of course, she was equal to any task. And it was good to see how, under sail, she 'stood up to the fresh breeze with the firmness of a rock, and sped along through a mist of spray...with every stitch of canvas set'.

What extraordinary powers of endurance these boats – and indeed their crews – would display! When Richard Williams of Cae Iago, Borth-y-Gest, put to sea in the *Sidney Smith* in June 1899, he would not return to his beloved home for two and a half years. Back and forth, back and forth across the globe: Cadiz, St John's, Newfoundland, Labrador, St Petersburg, South America; with coal, fish, salt, valonia, raw hides, linseed oil-cake... 32,000 miles.

The maritime custodian will tell such stories! Images will loom so

Opposite: A marina for Porthmadog! The harbour's pontoons will provide berths for 25 additional boats.

MADOC MAID

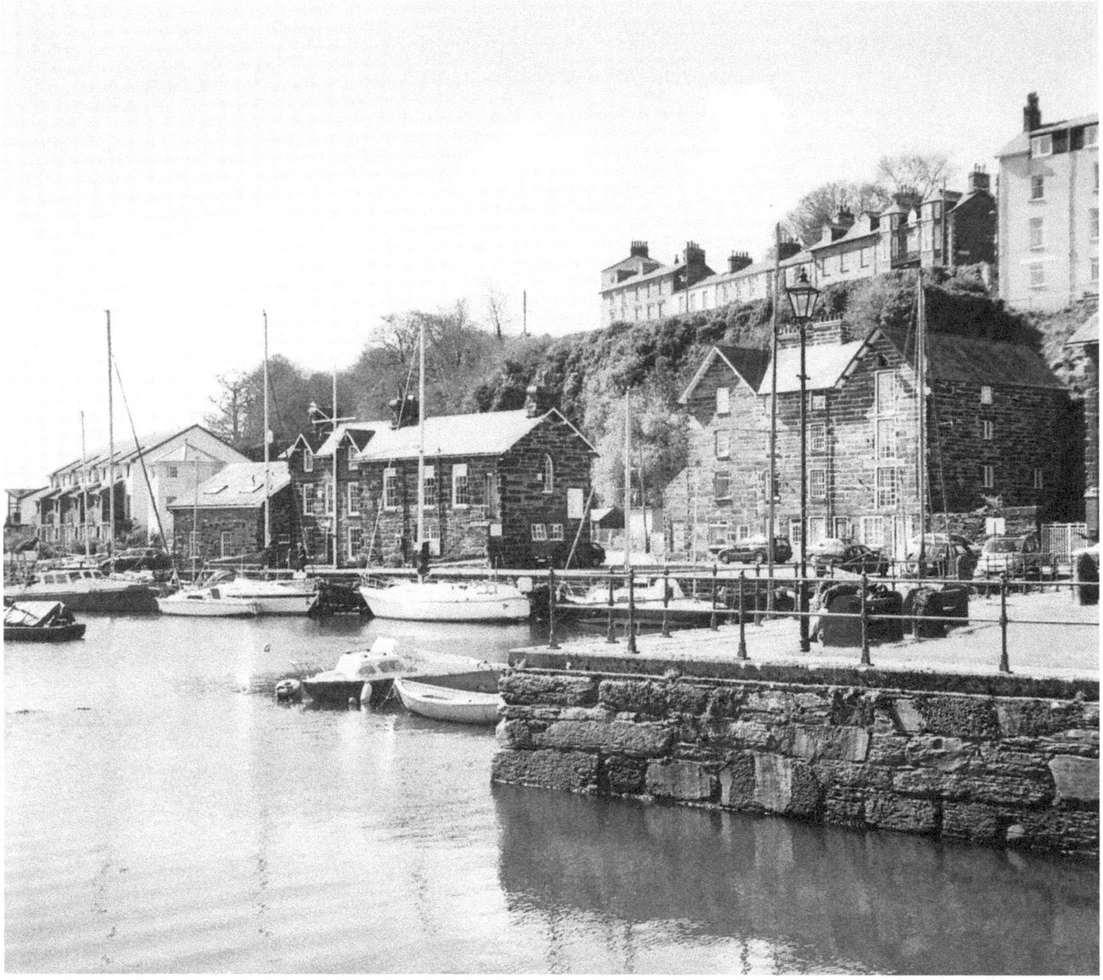

The harbour today.

Peter Leslie

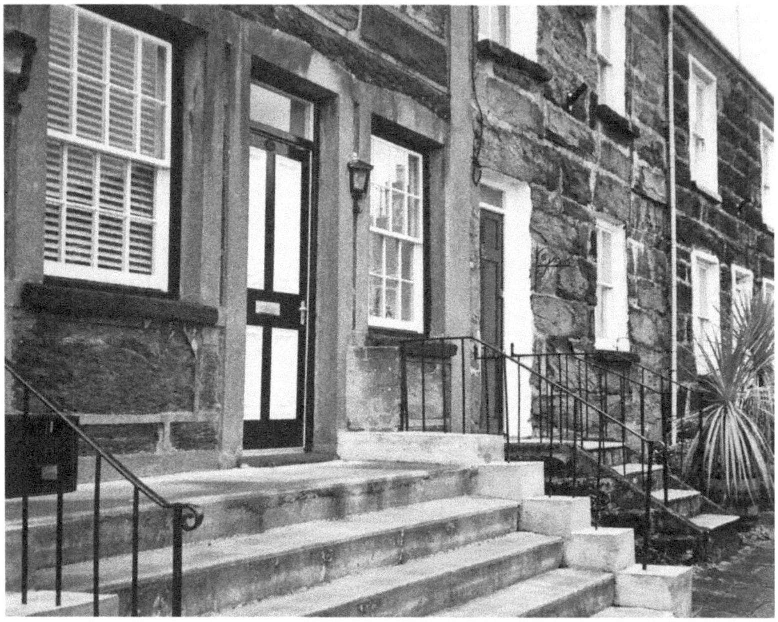

Cottages at Pencei.

Peter Leslie

Porthmadog harbour station. An old slate train with its diesel companion.

Oliver Hodgson

large that when you step out of the museum and into the daylight, you will believe yourself stalked by the very shadows of the ships and the men who sailed them!

Then look downstream, past the Yacht Club, and past the builders' and chandlers' yards that busily clutter the old slate wharves, and see how what was once a naked pile of rocks dumped in the stream from the outposts of the world has acquired a dressing of trees, even perhaps a slightly dreamy quality: how Ballast Island has become, in maturity, an Arcadian folly.

Cornhill, picturesque and atmospheric, retains a certain charm: a cobbled square, 'Victorian' lamp posts, tall, dark, handsome buildings… and the famous Grisiau Mawr – The Great Staircase – a tremendous flight of 83 stone steps, ringing with the footfalls of the past and leading upwards, through the old red-light district, to Portmadoc's earliest villas.

Before you climb to the top, however, there are two things to be done. One: treat yourself to a snack at Tafarn Pen Cei or the Ship (the town's oldest inn), and two: pop over to Browser's, the bookshop, and purchase a copy of *Immortal Sails* by Henry Hughes.

Winstay, Y Garth.

Opposite: Looking down on the world from Y Garth. A steam train from Blaenau Ffestinog pulls in to the harbour station.

III Y Garth

At the top of the great steps, Y Garth – the site of Portmadoc's earliest villas – exudes an air of quiet refinement. Known originally as Y Tywyn or Traeth, her initial names pre-dated that of Portmadoc itself. Thrice blessed by healthy detachment from, convenient proximity to, and enviable elevation above the port – Garth represents an unrivalled location.

Residential development began here in the early 1820s. It progressed rapidly, and by the 1850s the area could boast at least 200 houses. From the very outset, the novelty of Garth's position ensured that she would quickly become a most fashionable district and, even as her first villas took shape, they were eagerly adopted by the most prominent members of the new order: sea captains, ship owners, bankers and the like.

Garth's spectacular situation was something to cherish, for not only could her residents comfortably witness a port in the making, but they could also observe movements of river, sea and tide, formations of clouds and storms, and the changing moods of the great mountains of Eryri. And, furthermore, removed from the hectic rituals and events below, they could, if they so desired, simply shield their eyes from streets and wharves, and turn instead to the terraced gardens they had made on their hillside.

Yet those of a more curious nature could revel in their position of visual omniscience, for Garth was a window on the world, a window upon revolution, fit for the most studious individual.

But what of the village itself? If you had lived there, you may have been aware of the birth of Eliseus Williams and marvelled at his metamorphosis into Eifion Wyn, celebrated poet. Did you perhaps worship at the chapel (now demolished) in its glory days? Did you ever have tea with Sybil Thorndike and Hugh Casson at 'Bron-y-Garth'? Or were they seldom there? How did you respond to the blasting away of the headland of Clogwyn-y-Pig and the destruction of its romantic footpath?

And, speaking of romance! Given a harbour view such as yours, it would not have been surprising had you occasionally entertained romantic notions of sail and

The schooner *Catharine of Portmadoc.*

Cath Hope

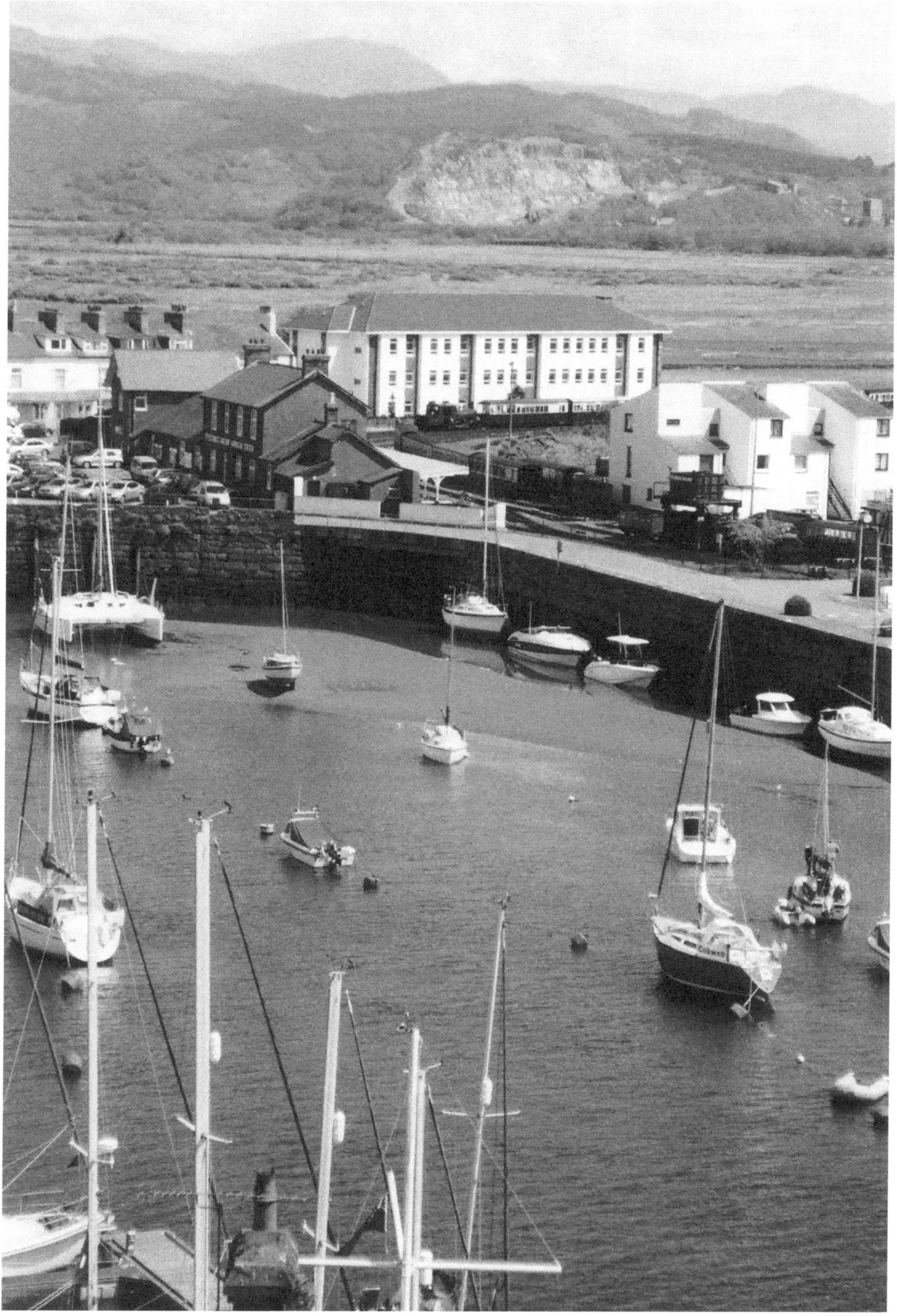

A gravestone in the cemetery in memory of five children of John Jones, tailor of Portmadoc.

Peter Leslie

sea. Heroic deeds, groaning timbers, broad billows of the open ocean and crimson sunsets on ultimate horizons. The very stuff of romance! Yet you must have been aware of an antithesis... the epitaphs in the village's cemetery for instance... to Captain Griffith Roberts, 'lost on passage from Cardiff to Portmadoc', and his sons William and Henry 'who died in infancy'; to William Jones, Master of the Schooner *Fossile*, aged 29, his wife Margaret, 32, their daughter Elizabeth, 13 months, and son John, seven years; to the four sons and daughter of John and Mary Thomas, 'their united age 12 years'.

Romantic notions in terrible perspective.

Promenade: Porthmadog to Borth-y-Gest

It is no more than a stone's throw from Porthmadog to Borth-y-Gest, yet this little seaside village inhabits a different world from its noisy neighbour. Notwithstanding an abundance of seasonal visitors, it remains unhurried, its residents courteous and relaxed.

If you are coming in to Borth on foot from Porthmadog Harbour, walk past the Yacht Club and along the lane beside the old slate quays – boatyards on the left. If, on the other hand, you have braved the 83 steps of Grisiau Mawr, turn seaward at the top and continue along the road until you find the village below you, blinking through the trees. A few steps will lead down to the shore. By car, you will have to turn into Bank Place and fork left down Borth Road at the top of the hill.

The pilot houses. Cath Hope

IV Borth-y-Gest

What will be seen (at least, according to a 1950s guide to North Wales) is a 'tiny replica of the Bay of Naples'! Be that as it may, the inlet is sheltered and shallow: a few boats standing stork-like on the sand at low tide; an arcing promenade bordered by villas and cottages – white, pink, delicate blues and greens; houses stepped-up on the hills behind. And, at the apex of the bay, in pride of place, the chapel of Ebenezer, 1880, seemingly protective of the dwellings that fan out from its walls. There is a pleasant tea room and a good restaurant. On the shore: parallel crescents of sand, shingle and mud, and – again when the tide is low – the Afon Glaslyn meandering past the threshold of the bay, seeking confluence with the Dwyryd.

The brig *Fleetwing*.

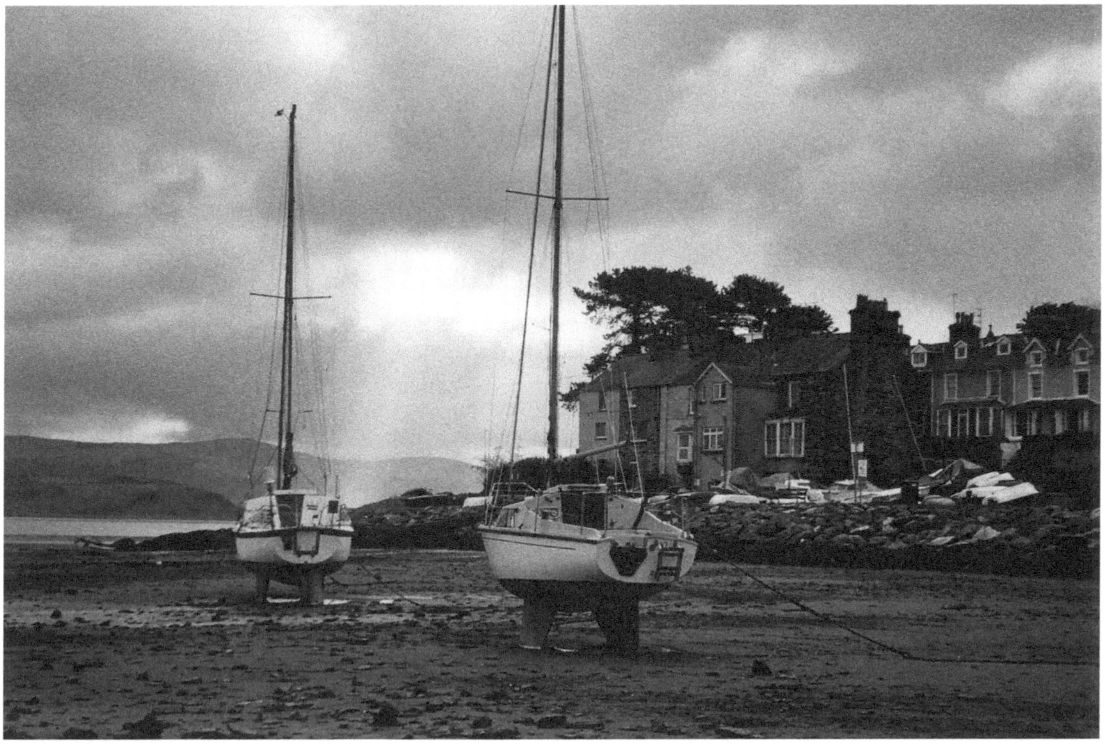

Early evening, Borth-y-Gest.

Borth-y-Gest. Jim Mowat

Stroll along the promenade and across the car park to the southern elbow of the bay. Pause for a few moments at Captain Williams's wooden bench – the old pilot houses behind you – and survey the scene: the Great Beach, shifting sands and drifting channels; a counterfeit lighthouse on Penrhyn shores; hazy mountains.

There was a time when a hundred boats would pass the mouth of this bay. The Borth pilots would heave away from the slipway, to meet and guide a late arrival to safety. The barque *Snowdonia* would lie, half complete, on the blocks before you, and, a couple of hundred yards across the shingle, Richard Jones, hands on hips, would inspect the frame of his near-finished *Fleetwing*.

PROMENADE:
BORTH-Y-GEST TO CRICIETH

But, it is time to move on...

Leave Borth-y-Gest by way of the steps beside the pilot houses. Turn left and soon, near St Cyngar's Church, the lane gives way to a grassy knoll. A coastal path[5], winding and dipping through dune and wood, will lead – via rocks, red and white – to the province of the wandering minstrel Dafydd y Garreg Wen, to Ynys Cyngar – the harbour of the Philistines – and to the seemingly boundless sands of Graig Ddu, Black Rock.

Black Rock Sands is among Penrhyn Llŷn's best tourist beaches: long,

St Cyngar's Church.
Jim Mowat

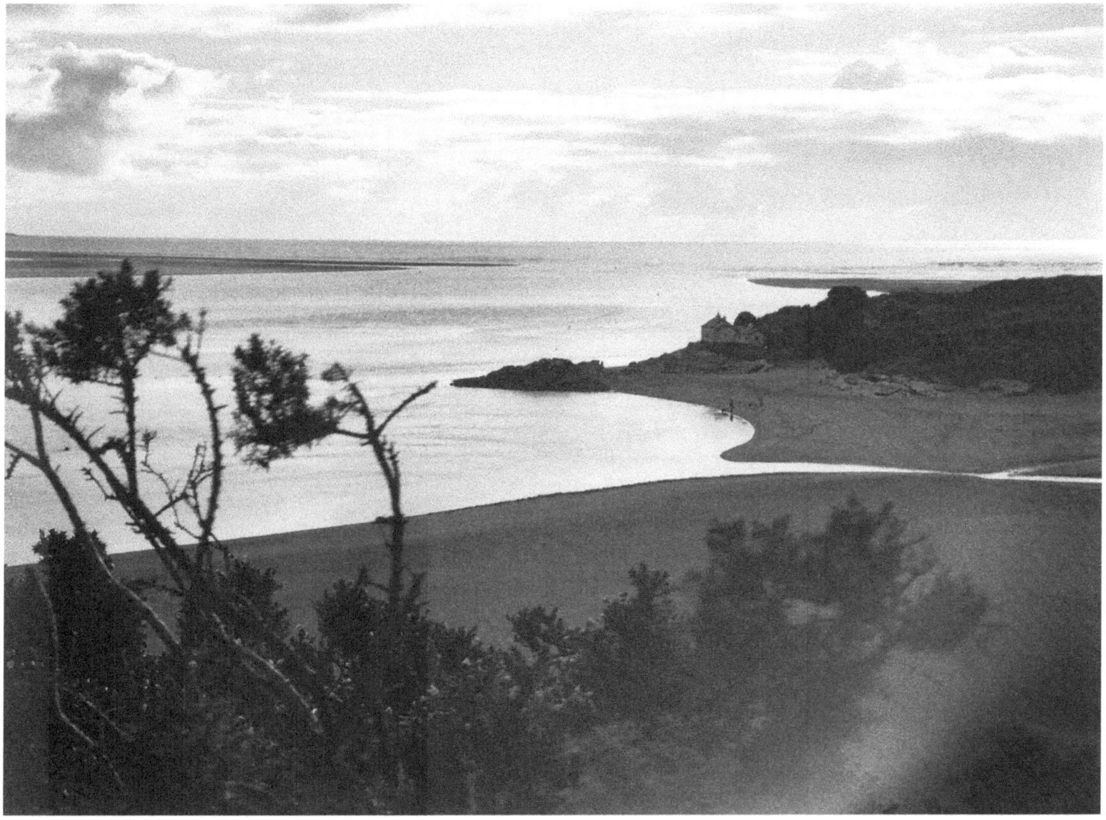

Looking south-west towards Ynys Cyngar.

firm, golden, safe and motor-friendly, it is a brisk-walking, wave-splashing, fit-keeping sort of place. Facing Harlech and the Rhinog mountains, skimmed by gulls, ringed by sand dunes, and by a large (but discreet) conurbation of holiday parks, its supremacy is hard to dispute.

At the west end of the beach, Graig Ddu – Black Rock itself – seems impassable; determined, apparently, to impede further progress. Clearly, even at low tide, there is no way round to the south, and the facing wall is sheer. Fortunately, however, the rock's intransigence is but an illusion, for in truth, a number of passages are there for the taking: a scramble over the headland's lower slopes, a ramble across high meadows or, by car, an inland diversion – via St Michael's Church, the pilgrims' church, at Treflys[6] and the fairy-tale wood of Chwarel – to the main Pwllheli road.

Cricieth from Rhiw.

rhiw.com

V Cricieth

From the high meadows, a winding farm track leads back to the shore. Ahead, a defining image! The splendid ruins of Cricieth Castle reclining on its rocky plinth. Castle and rock as one, a synthesis of nature, architect and history. Seen from the east bay, this is a classic view, a view captured by countless artists over the centuries. In

Cricieth Castle 'Wales's friendliest'.

the 1830s Turner painted it – highly dramatised with half-drowned sailors and mounted coast guards. And truly, it is a worthy subject. For even the most insentient observer could not fail to acclaim its geometry and balance; its horizon, emphatic or uncertain according to moment; its promontory and fortress crown, ablaze with sunlight or deep in shadow; the sea, angrily lashing groyne and jetty, or harmlessly lapping sand and pebble. Cottages clinging to the slope of Lôn Felin, a glimpse of y Drêf – the old town – between castle gate and rocky Dinas.

Jan Morris describes Cricieth Castle as 'Wales's friendliest', standing there as it does on its promontory 'in the middle of the little resort as though it was put there for purely ornamental purposes'.[7] And yes, it does have the look of a good-natured old soul, but history tells a different story.

Built in the 13th century by Llywelyn Fawr (Llywelyn the Great), the castle was regarded as a formidable prison. Rebellions and plots infested its walls. In 1283 it fell into English hands and, though King Edward I had no wish to make of it a Caernarfon or a Conwy, it became a royal garrison of sufficient consequence to receive the King and his entourage on several occasions.

A year later – brazenly many would argue – Edward creates 'Crukyth' an English Borough and, for a time at least, stability prevails. A town hall and market, a number of cottages, a tax office and village stocks assume their positions in the lee of the castle, beside the King's bakery and the treasury's 'Gate of Gold'. Farther afield, on the borough's

The castle in the early years of the 20th century.
Anne and Henry Roberts

wooded slopes, grand English burgesses choose their estates and commission fine houses. It is a well-ordered community...

But beware you Englishmen! It is now 1400 and Owain Glyndŵr is at large. He will sweep west and besiege your castle. Its stones will be engulfed in dragon's fire. All around anarchy will threaten, prestigious families will make war and the land will be stained with blood... Cricieth Castle will never be rebuilt, but will stand forever as a memorial to this extraordinary moment.

One hundred years later, on his Welsh travels, John Leland will come to Cricieth and declare the village 'clere decayed'.

But history is eternal motion! Seasons spin, decay is reversed and in its time, Cricieth rises again. Fishing boats bring herring to the jetty, and Abermarchnad – the lively market at the foot of Lôn Felin – echoes to the banter and curses of traders and their haggling customers; coal and timber clutter the harbour walls and limestone-stacked carts trundle to the quayside from the kiln across the square. Cricieth, the working village, enjoys a degree of prosperity.

Eternal motion: and on another day – though not for some time yet – the borough will be drawn into changes so fundamental as to shift its very heart and redefine its purpose. Two factors – a road and a railway – will effect this transformation.

The turnpike road from Tremadoc to Porth Dinllaen – the core of William Madocks's Irish ambitions – will slice through Cricieth in 1809. It will create a new high street and – around the Maes – a centre so dynamic that gradually, Abermarchnad and Y Drêf will be starved of activity. Cricieth will be turned upside down.

The Cambrian Railway will surge along the shores of Eifionydd and Llŷn in the 1860s. Reaching Cricieth in 1867, it will introduce new opportunities and concepts, particularly in an embryonic age of sea bathing and hill walking. In so doing it will question the village's future.

Not that Cricieth had stagnated during the decades between

Strolling into town.

The Marine Terrace.

Sepiatone

turnpike and railway. Her population had continued to grow (it stood at 900 in 1870), and her buildings had continued to spread. She had good inns, commodious chapels, and a happy equation of decent cottages and fine houses. And, although as late as 1878 her 'comfortable lodgings' were said to be 'not numerous', she was by no means unknown to the visitor.

But in the 1870s visitors were beginning to arrive in increasing numbers. Hotels were being built on Marine Terrace to accommodate them. It was decision time! Should Cricieth embrace 'the holiday maker' or not? If yes, would she be willing to compromise her character in order to do so, and by how much? If not, how might she justify shunning such a potentially profitable engagement?

An affirmative answer would require Cricieth to adopt unfamiliar attitudes and practices. She must learn to see herself through the eyes of others and must consider – in a way she has never done before – her appearance. She must become less self-effacing, must flatter and charm. She must place a price upon things which, as a working community, she will hardly have noticed: the efficacy of her climate, the quality of her air, the generosity of her sunlight, the lushness of her vegetation, the translucence of her water. Even the 'timelessness' of her atmosphere. She must regard a crumbling castle, lying in disarray, as a romantic prodigy, a prosaic harbour wall as a magical vantage point, a simple beach as a health-inducing, recreational wonderland. She must create 'facilities': hotels to indulge, tea rooms to seduce, shops to entice, beach huts to shield, a theatre to divert. She must trim her lawns and put flowers in her streets. Her spectacular location must be reappraised and tendered as a thing of beauty. And when Hillaire Belloc climbs Castle Hill and looks out across the mountains, he must be inspired to write that there is nowhere in Europe 'which so moves me with the awe and majesty of great things as does this mass of the northern Welsh mountains seen from this corner of their silent sea'.[8]

The commitment is made! And before long, Cricieth, the 'most salubrious of resorts', will be carried aloft, wreathed in approval…

Exceptionally well-favoured by nature, views of sea and mountain unsurpassed in extent and grandeur by any other resort in Britain, Cricieth in the Land of the Golden Gorse, long-favoured by the medical faculty, held in high repute as a health resort, excellent sanitation, water pure and plentiful, sheltered from the cold north and east winds, renewed by the warm south-westerly breezes set in motion by the Gulf Stream, spring flowers a-bloom in January, fig, myrtle, fuchsia and hydrangea flourishing throughout the winter. Cricieth: elegant, fashionable; sailing, tennis, golf, bathing; beaches to the east and west, the one leading the eye to the great mountains, the other, it seems, to infinity; Mediterranean light, peace and seclusion.

As time went by it became clear that Cricieth had worked a miracle, for not only had she achieved her distinction without losing her integrity, but she had even managed somehow to please both visitor and resident. And so it is today. Fine shops and restaurants, good hotels and tea rooms, homely cottages and leisured villas. She has festivals and country fairs, music, drama and streets filled with flowers.

Caffi Cwrt –'ty té'.

The sweep of Cricieth Bay... 'exceptionally well-favoured by nature'.

But, forgive me! To have abandoned you – castle-struck – on the east foreshore is unpardonable. Let us move on...

Leave the shore at Café Moranedd – one of Williams-Ellis's more modest creations – and walk along the Esplanade to the Blue China Café and the little square where Abermarchnad once stood: to your right, the old village mill (now a gallery) and Cricieth's fine lifeboat house; to your left, on the shore, slipways old and new clasped together, a stern jetty, and Bonzo Jones's boat shed. There's a grassy outcrop nearby where you might relax and enjoy a Cadwalader's secret recipe ice cream, or, should it be a summer Sunday, perhaps join the assembled hymn singers and lift your voice to Heaven. You could even meet a sea captain.

A cottage on the Maes.

Peter Leslie

The Blue China tearooms.

Take a seat – Blue China and Moelwyn behind you – and look out across the glassy water towards the rest of the world. An old man in sea captain's hat and brass-buttoned blazer sits beside you. Conversation, or at least oratory, comes easily to him. Born in Cricieth 85 years ago, he once lived in the village's oldest cottage on Wellington Terrace. He fished and sailed from here. He mended boats and helped shape the course of the Afon Wdad, which flows down under the road. He can well remember the old lime kiln and the long-gone hotels of the Esplanade, not to mention the Abermarchnad cottages that were swept

Bonzo Jones, fisherman and sage.

away by the sea in 1927. He points towards Lôn Felin: 'Bird's Custard House', destined forever to be painted either yellow or pink; he recalls the great aunt who worked at the butcher's shop in Y Drêf and served Lloyd George with tasty chops and legs of lamb; the great man's solicitor's office on Tan-y-Grisiau… and – in case you ask – no, he never did meet Lloyd George, but – as you may guess – his father did! Moreover, in the 1880s his grandfather once bumped into Rider Haggard outside the Castle Bakery. Haggard was apparently staying at one of the George's houses in Cricieth, and could well have been putting the

The Castell Tea Rooms, now 'No.29'.

Cath Hope

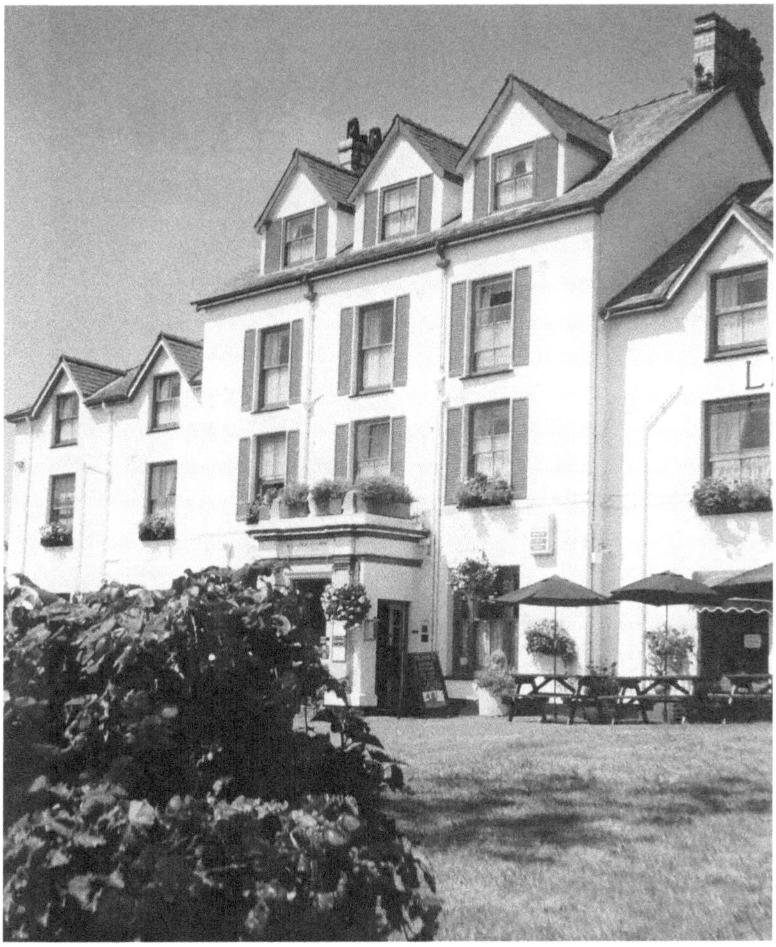

The Lion Hotel in the centre of Cricieth.

Opposite: Y Traeth, Cricieth.

finishing touches to *King Solomon's Mines*. The captain continues, allowing no intervention, a seamless off-by-heart stream of tales. Practised, plausible. And the next moment he is gone, pottering down Beach Bank.

Lôn Felin, rich in historical prizes, is dominated by the towers of the castle – mighty from this perspective – and its attendant houses. Entering the confines of Y Drêf – clustered cottages, cautious doorways, inquisitive windows – it is hard to deny a sense of its shadowy past.

For an unparalleled view of Cricieth you may climb Dinas from here… the castle rising from the rooftops of the old town, the inns on the turnpike, Capel Mawr, the Maes sloping obligingly and tapering towards the sea, and, in a distant corner, ancient and mysteriously situated, St Catherine's Church. You may be struck by Cricieth's visual harmony, by the lie of the land, the buildings old and new which snuggle into her contours without let or hindrance.[9]

Promenade:
Cricieth to Llanystumdwy

Walk now along Marine Terrace and head west over the boulder-tossed beach towards the mouth of the Afon Dwyfor. As the tide ebbs, look at the reflections in the polished stones and see how the bony groynes divide the waves.

Follow the curve of the river for a short distance. The way ahead is marshy, sometimes excessively so. It might be sensible, therefore, to

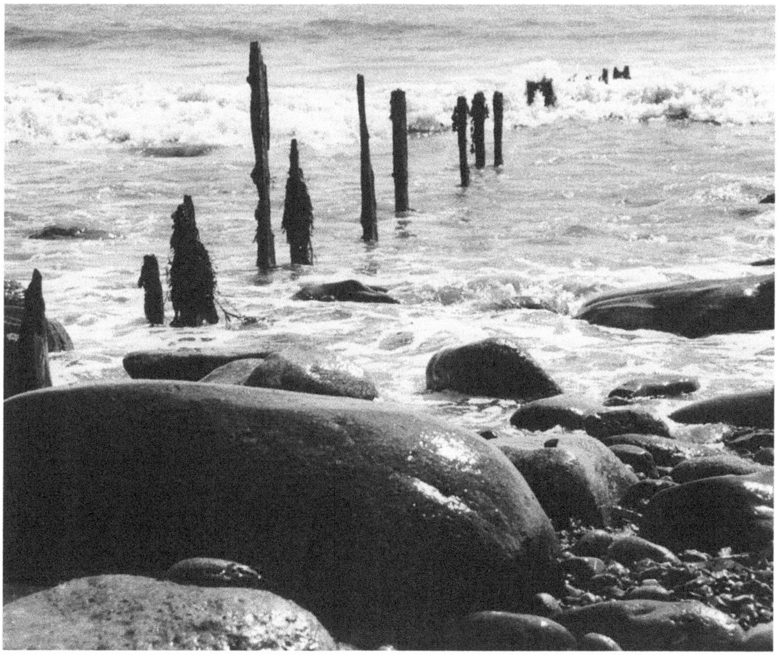

The beach to the west.

Peter Leslie

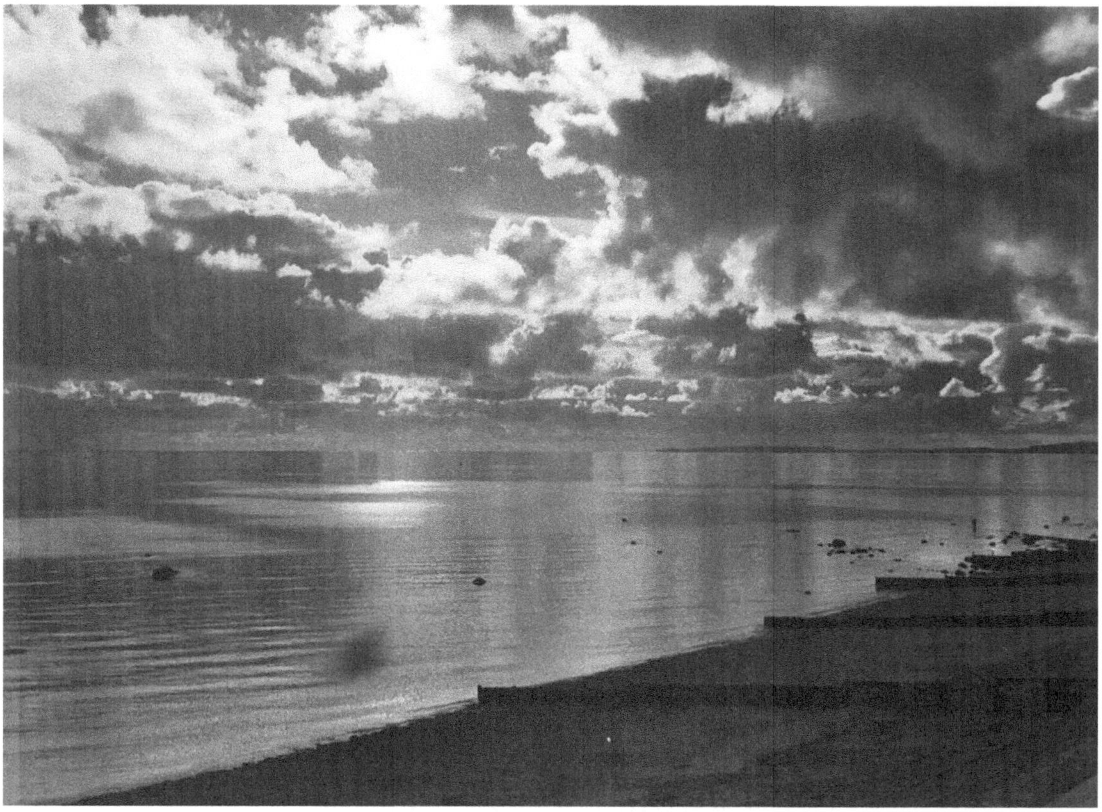

Looking towards Pen-y-Chain from Marine Terrace.

move inland as soon as possible. Turn right beside the fishermen's huts on the edge of the marsh. There is an open gateway here, and the path will take you, via a house called 'Dwyfor', to the main road. Turn left, and then turn right at the sign for Llanystumdwy.

Should you continue through the marsh and along the river, however, turn right at the new kissing gate, since straight ahead there is no convenient river crossing. And be not confused by the signpost to Llwybr Cyhoeddus… for it means public footpath!

VI Lloyd George's village

St John's Church and the bridge over the Afon Dwyfor.

Llanystumdwy – Lloyd George's village – is typically described as 'sleepy'. But of course, that all depends.You may indeed come to the village on a sleepy day, a spring afternoon, say. There may be hardly anyone about, except for a couple of visitors sipping tea under a sunshade at the riverside café, and Gwilym the gardener cycling slowly, silently by.

But 'sleepy'? On another day, listen to the rumpus as the junior football team surges to victory in that crucial cup match, or share the excitement as children and adults alike fuss and chatter, making ready

The village school, Llanystumdwy.

for their annual carnival procession to Cricieth and back. Hear music flooding from the village hall, or the expectant twittering of ragamuffins waiting outside the Lloyd George museum for their visit to the Victorian classroom. Behold the lawn of the Dwyfor café on a warm Bank Holiday Monday, or an evening barbecue at Tafarn Y Plu, the village inn. Sleepy's not the word.

Round about Llanystumdwy the land undulates gently and unsensationally. From the spring woods – freshly green and not yet dense – tiny streams trickle or percolate down to join the Afon Dwyfor as it picks its way discreetly between the ancient stones that form its bed.

Gwynfor and Dorothy Hughes, proprietors of the riverside Dwyfor Café, sponsors of Llanystumdwy Football Club, seen here with the inaugural team of 1989–90.

The ever-popular Dwyfor Café.
Cath Hope

Today the water is low and almost still, and it is hard to imagine the forces of which it is sometimes capable. Soon the clear crystal pools that mark its course will be rippling with salmon and sea trout, but not for a few days yet, for it is well known that the fish will not come here until the foxgloves are in flower, after the Cricieth fair.

On a boulder beside this river, Lloyd George would sit and meditate. As a boy he would paddle here and scramble for eels along the river bank, and although, when the time came, he would leave Llanystumdwy

The Afon Dwyfor at Llanystumdwy.

'Highgate', the boyhood home of Lloyd George.

Photochrom

'Highgate' today.

'Ty Newydd', David Lloyd George's last home. Recently refurbished and extended, the house is now the National Writers Centre for Wales.

'without regret', he would return again and again to these childhood haunts. He would walk here with Winston Churchill, and one can only imagine what schemes were hatched in these peaceful woods. And when he was old, he would retire to 'Ty Newydd' – a farmhouse not a quarter of a mile from 'Highgate', his childhood home – and the river would provide his title: Earl Lloyd George of Dwyfor. He would die close to it and be buried beside it, the boulder his memorial. Churchill would remember him as 'the greatest Welshman which that unconquerable race has produced since the Tudors', and some years later, the Queen would visit his grave to pay her respects.

Lloyd George as a young man.

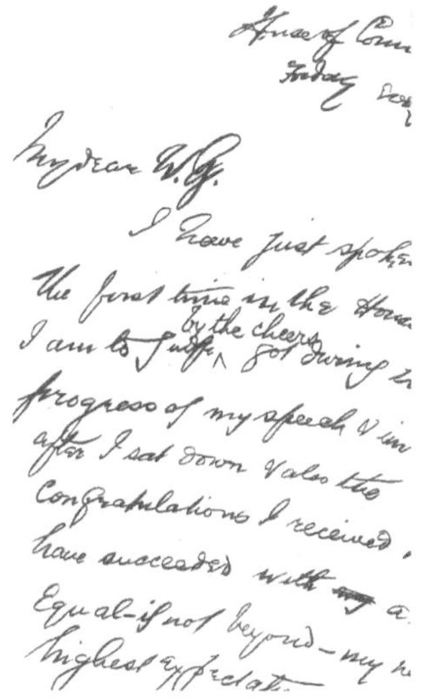
House of Com
Friday
My dear W.G.
I have just spok
the first time in the Hou
I am to judge by the cheers I got during
progress of my speech & im
after I sat down & also the
congratulations I received
have succeeded with a
Equal – if not beyond – my
highest expectat–

I have just spoken for the first time in the House and if I am to judge by the cheers I got during the progress of my speech and immediately after I sat down... I must have succeeded with a success equal – if not beyond – my highest expectations.

The grave of Lloyd George, overlooking his beloved river.

Peter Leslie

The Moriah Chapel from the grounds of the Lloyd George Museum.

ONE LIFE

It is the summer of 1953. A coronation is eagerly anticipated. The nation is optimistic, the press ebullient. It is the dawn of a new era. Yet when, on the morning of the great day, the *Times* appears, it is a quite different story that thrills its readers. One of epic human endurance: the conquest of Everest. What a sublime coincidence: it is 2 June, the birth of a new Elizabethan Age, and a British-led expedition commandeers the roof of the world! The timely disclosure of this heroic deed is the work of a young correspondent, James Morris, who has accompanied the expedition from first to last. Katmandu, Khumba, the silent Cwm; through ice-field and avalanche, disappointment and exhilaration, to the final 'weary triumph'. He has demonstrated amazing resilience and enterprise.

James Morris will one day become Jan Morris, 'the greatest living travel writer in the world'.[10] A handsome compliment indeed, but an inadequate one even so. Historian, novelist, philosopher, traveller, story-teller, she is all of these. And more again.

One recalls an evening spent in her company at Capel Moriah, Llanystumdwy, not so long ago.[11] She spoke about 'outsiders', special people who had in one way or another touched her life. Afterwards – such is the affection in which she is held – the lawns of the chapel were crowded with folk eager to shake her hand. For above all, notwithstanding her fame and her journeys, Jan Morris is gloriously local.

She lives, with her life-long partner Elizabeth, in a lovely old house 'Trefan Morys', not far from the village, above the Afon Dwyfor. If you should pass by on the lane and happen to see her in the garden, she will not think twice about inviting you in for a cup of tea. And maybe she will tell you, for she likes to do so, how 'Trefan Morys' embodies – in the indigenous stones of which it is composed – the substance and indeed the very spirit of Wales.[12]

In due course she and Elizabeth will be buried on a small island in the river below. She prepared their gravestone long ago. It reads:

Yma mae dwy ffrind
Jan & Elizabeth Morris,
Ar derfyn un bywyd

Here are two friends
Jan & Elizabeth Morris,
At the end of one life.

Promenade:
Llanystumdwy to Pwllheli

It is easy, if you are so inclined, to 'escape' Llanystumdwy. Tracks and lanes lead off in every direction, to shore, secret village, mountain. To Bron Eifion – hotel, nursery, fishing pools – to Dragon Raiders, Ranch and Rabbit Farm.

As for the beach, a meadow path from Bont Fechan – the tiny bridge across the Dwyfach – will take you to the long, unadorned shingle fringe south of the village. Here, beyond the meeting of Dwyfor and Dwyfach, the coast can feel strangely remote. In any case, the shore towards Porth Fechan is not especially hospitable and, since the Afon Wen may be awkward to negotiate, it may be prudent to choose an inland route to Pen-y-Chain.

Pen-y-Chain, the headland of Oxen, the fabled headland of sighs. And once the headland of bathing beauties and redcoats, knobbly knees, sausages and chips. Yes, it was close to these sheltered coves and

Cooks and redcoats, entertainers, gardeners, maids and managers, all at your service! The staff of Butlin's Holiday camp in the late 1950s.

Menorcan-blue waters that Billy Butlin established his famous 'Pwllheli' Holiday Camp. It was 1947. What a moment that must have been for a shell-shocked Britain! Built on the site of a former naval base – where Prince Philip served – Butlin's represented fun, laughter and even romance to hundreds of thousands of holidaymakers for the next 50 years. Inevitably, as tastes changed, Butlin's – a small gem of social history – became easy to mock. It has gone now of course, and has been superseded (if not replaced) by a splendid Hafan y Môr, Haven of the Sea, Holiday Park. But memories linger.

To the west of Pen-y-Chain, three or four high terraces of shingle oppose the wildest seas before gradually petering out into a long, sandy beach, more golden at every step and backed by silver-green dunes. You will soon pass Abererch, and as the beach curves to the south a little before Glan Môr 'Berch, you will be close – closer than you might think – to Pwllheli, the capital of Llŷn.

A busy day for the main station at Abererch!

Penarth Fawr, a beautifully restored mediaeval hall-house near Afon Wen, is under the care of CADW, the organisation responsible for the upkeep and protection of Wales's historic monuments.

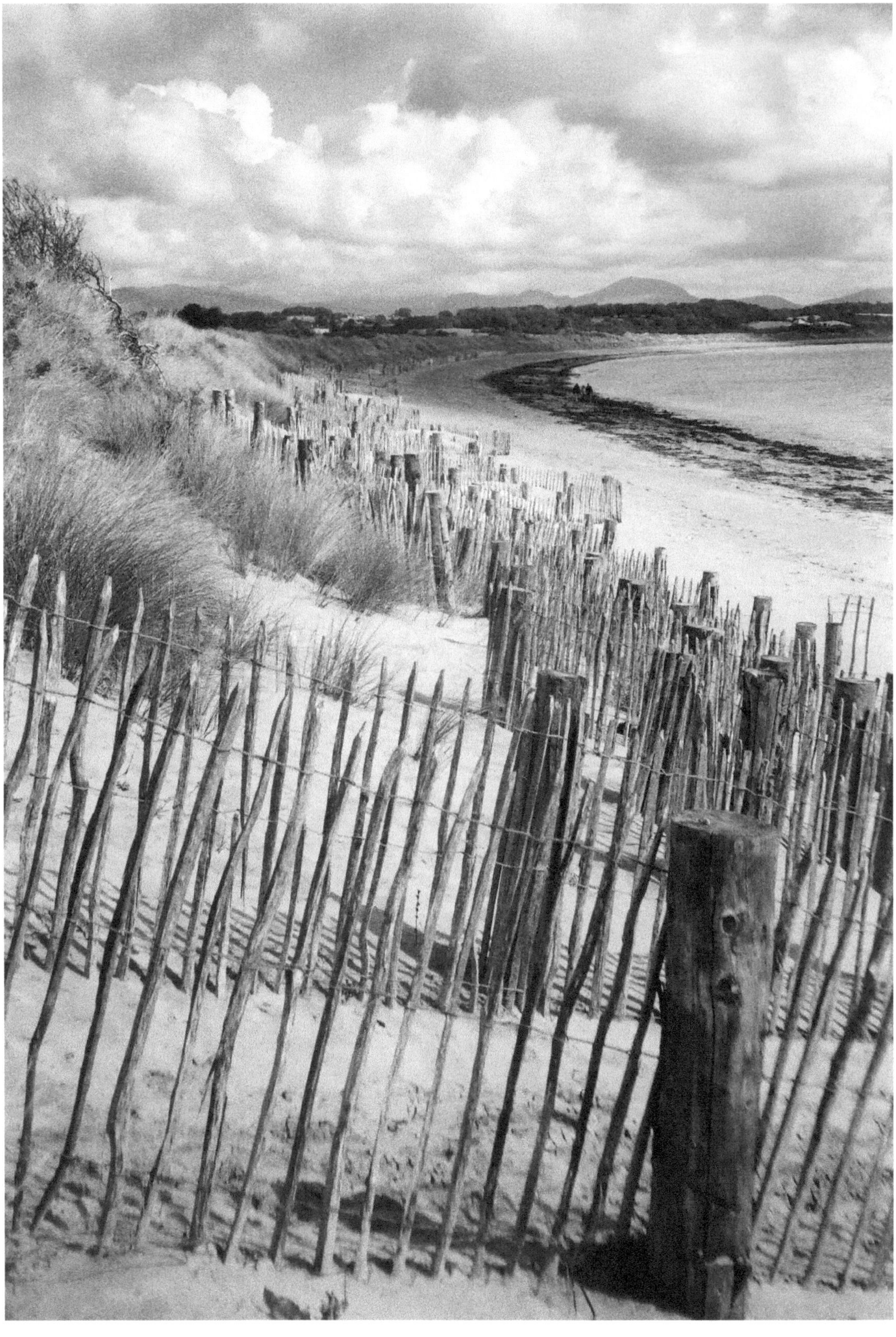

Part II Llŷn and Arfon

Opposite: The beach, looking back to Abererch.

Peter Leslie

VII Pwllheli

Leave the beach by the broad slipway and head towards the harbour. You may be surprised. For nothing – certainly not the artless sands of Glan Môr 'Berch – will have prepared you for its splendour. It reaches out towards you and opens up before you like a cupboard filled with wonderful toys. Look at the marina – Yr Hafan – and marvel! Dazzling yachts trimmed with silver thread, palatial Chaparrals and Fairlines, boats, workshops and boatyards as far as the eye can see, countless ranks of Mercedes with dark windows and a handsome club house, perched on the quayside, well versed in the arcane procedures of international regatta and champagne reception. It is said that the businesses here contribute £20 million a year to the local economy, and proposals for expansion have long been under scrutiny. They are deeply controversial.

Pwllheli, the capital of Llyn.

Catriona and Rodney Bracewell

LH152. Ever faithful.

Peter Leslie

Pwllheli is passionately Welsh. Cymraeg, the first language of 80 percent of the region's population, is no romantic abstraction here. It is the language 'of the hearth' and of discourse; of thought, poetry, prayer and breath. It is the language of 'Welshness' – Cymreictod – the cultural sum of Llŷn.

In the modern world, however, ancient languages and traditions are easily overwhelmed. To many in the region, therefore, the survival of Welsh culture is the mainspring of life.

'Hafan Pwllheli', the clubhouse.

The impassioned word, the defiant gesture, have distinguished Pwllheli's history. The first-ever weekly Welsh language newspaper was printed here, the *Trumpet of Freedom* (*Yr Udgorn Rhyddid*) sounded in these very streets, and Sir Albert Evans-Jones – thrice-crowned Archdruid Cynan – was born here. This is the town visited three times by the National Eisteddford of Wales, and it is where ,in 1925 – on the occasion of the second of these visits – Lloyd George's impassioned words stirred the sleeping dragon of Cymreictod. It was here in the same year that six men came together in a hotel on the Maes and formed Plaid Cymru, the Party of Wales, and it was not far from here that three of those six – D.J. Williams, Saunders Lewis and Lewis Valentine – set fire to an RAF bombing school and were jailed for the defiant gesture.

UDGORN RHYDDID.

(The Trumpet of Freedom)

Newyddiadur Cenedlaethol Cymreig.

RHIF 51. CYF. II. DYDD MERCHER, RHAGFYR 19, 1888. Pris Dimai.

Y CYNGOR SIROL.

CYNGHOR SIROL

At Etholwyr Sirol Dosbarth Llanengan a Llangian.

ACHOS CLADDU LLANFROTHEN.

MARWOLAETH MR. ROBERT OWEN, PWLLHELI.

The Trumpet of Freedom, title page, 1888. Inset: Lloyd George, young parliamentarian.

Though time has passed, passions still run high. It is hardly surprising, then, that proposals for the expansion of the marina – from 420 to over 700 berths – were regarded as unacceptable by some members of the community. For while supporters claimed that the development would promote further economic growth, create new jobs and student training schemes, encourage tourism and enhance the town's status in sailing and the marine crafts, opponents predicted catastrophe: pollution, inflated house prices, and, most importantly, the encouragement of a climate detrimental to indigenous language and culture.

The argument dragged on for several years. Decisions were made, suspended, unmade, and, as frustrations multiplied, rational debate gave way to personal recrimination and rhetoric. The project was abandoned in 2005, the 650th anniversary of the foundation of this vehement maritime town, only to reappear a year later. 'Plans for marina back on track', announced the *Herald* in November 2006. Yes? No? Maybe? Thus it shall continue for many a day!

Yet even at the height of the conflict, Pwllheli neither looked nor felt like a community divided. In the shops and cafés and on the streets, be you tourist or resident, young or old, it seemed to make no difference – there was apparently no disharmony. And, as far as language was concerned, Cymraeg and English (not to mention a good-natured hybrid of the two!) continued to co-exist with perfect ease.

Pwllheli's crest – elephant and castle.

Penmount, chapel and cottages.

From the Embankment of Glandon, look across the harbour towards the town. Pwllheli will seem a jumble: church spires, Neuadd Dwyfor glowing red, a whimsical clock tower, fitful rooftops, all heaped together in tight confusion. See how the angles scatter and re-form as North Quay looms. Here, too, are the annals of Pwllheli past… maritime chronicles pre-dating and at least equalling the glories of Porthmadog and Borth-y-Gest, and the spirits of the shipbuilders of Glandon, Y Traeth and Penmount. William Jones, master craftsman; David Williams of Abererch; Thomas Hughes from Penlan. Mr Pritchard attending the launch of his *Twelve Apostles*, unaware as yet of its terrible fate. The long shadow of *Margaret Pugh*, her near-mutiny far in the future. The souls of a thousand ships – sloops, brigs, barques – and of the mariners, anonymous, indispensable, who manned them. Here is

William Jones's timber yard, 1890.

rhiw.com

the Baltimore record-holder and the steamer *Rebecca* en route to Liverpool… 200 mile-a-day clippers; a noisy crowd inspecting Mr Richardson's tubular steel lifeboat – speculating, doubting. Everywhere, drifting silt and shifting banks; engineers probing, concocting harbours and cobs, reclaiming marsh, creating lands.

When you come to the North Quay, turn left and cross the blue bridge – the Afon Erch breaking free beneath. To one side the railway, to the other the harbour, and between them, an unlovely collection of sheds and yards. See the old town – older by far than its Prince's Charter – creeping inland towards the hills – Y Garn, Allt Fawr – and the new, spreading out towards the sea.

Lon Abererch. A backdrop of golden gorse.

Soon you will come to Pen Cei and the railway station – a 'temporary' building erected in 1909 when the Cambrian line was extended into the town centre from its original terminus east of the harbour. Turn left now and walk along the Cob towards the war memorial. The distant view to the east is quite magnificent: an ever-changing yet timeless panorama of Wales's greatest mountains – a 'horseshoe of charm' as Henry Hughes once said. Yr Wyddfa (Snowdon), Lliwedd, Moel Hebog, Moel Ddu, Cnicht, Moelwyn Mawr, Moelwyn Bach, Moel Ysgyfarnogod, Rhinog Fawr, Rhinog, Y Llethr and, deep in the south, Cader Idris.

Continuing along the Cob you will come to Ynys yn Harbour, once, but no longer, an island. There is a pleasant footpath here and fine views of town and harbour. Walk on towards the sea and you will discover the old lifeboat station of Tocyn Brwyn, the remains of the voraciously-quarried Carreg yr Imbill (Gimlet Rock), where 170 men once carved out granite sets for city streets, and the promenade and dunes of the recently-revived South Beach.

Turning back towards the town, spend a few peaceful moments among the sheltered pools and reed banks of Lôn Bach Cob, at once sequestered yet close to the madding crowd! Turn left at Station Square and you will come to the Maes.

The first 'sitting out'. The Mitre in early spring.

This is the heart of town. All roads lead here and, it seems, everyone comes here. Particularly on Wednesdays, when the square reclaims (from the ubiquitous motor car) its traditional role of market and meeting place. The Maes has a rich and varied history, and although it cannot claim to be the site of Pwllheli's earliest markets – indeed, it was a tidal marsh until the 1830s – it has, nonetheless, welcomed generations of circuses, religious and political meetings, not to mention the town's famous spring and autumn 'hiring' fairs.

Today it is the very place to obtain – at a good price – those special things in life: the 'Croeso' tea towel, the laser gun, the *Godfather* poster, the Berber 'runner' – as well as such essentials as 'flyswats', X-tra large trousers ('ladies a speciality') and Bob Jones's much yearned for Brisket of Welsh Black Beef. If you wish, you can spoil yourself here! Have a fling at Siop Betio, a fresh 'donut' at the Village Coffee Shop; or you may simply imbibe the atmosphere, enjoy the conversational buzz, inhale the scent of sizzling sausage, and heed the hoots and howls from the dodgems at the nearby fairground.

Gaol Street, Stryd Moch.
rhiw.com

To the north of the Maes, just across the street –

between Cornelius Roberts' Meat Store and the Mitre Inn – is the foot of Stryd Moch, an ideal starting point for a brief circular tour of central Pwllheli... Stryd Moch – Stryd Fawr – Stryd Penlan, a route which passes some of the town's most venerable features: Capel Penlan, its oldest chapel (famed for an association with hymn writer Ann Griffiths), the cellar gaol, hotels temperate and intemperate, the old corn market, town halls ancient and modern, Penlan Fawr – Pwllheli's oldest building – and a host of colourful little shops.[13]

'The Gimlet Rock', by A.R. Quinton.

rhiw.com

The Labours of Solomon

Pwllheli the port, Pwllheli the market town, and now Pwllheli of a third kind – the resort.

It is easy to pass through the town without knowing of its glorious beaches. This must be very disappointing to the ghost of Solomon Andrews.

The sands.

rhiw.com

Signs of the times. rhiw.com

In 1893 Mr Andrews visits Pwllheli. As a Victorian entrepreneur he is not amused. The town (notwithstanding a rail link with Llandudno, where Mr Andrews is enjoying a quiet holiday) is remote, and, to be blunt, somewhat dour. Development is sporadic, accommodation basic, the extensive harbour uneventful. Having been enticed to Pwllheli by the prospect of obtaining building land adjacent to the sea, he has so far observed little to excite his imagination. To make matters worse, it is not a particularly pleasant day, and his return train will not leave Pwllheli for two whole hours.

Mr Andrews's ill-humour, however, is short-lived. To pass the time (if our tale is to be believed) he walks along the Cob in the direction of what he discovers to be the South Beach Hotel. It is an engaging building, with arches, dormers and tall turrets, the centrepiece of a seaside development devised by three local men, David Evan Davies, Edward Jones and Robert Jones – the minister, the grocer and the bank manager. Occupying land reclaimed during the harbour improvement scheme, the so-called South Beach Estate is a relatively modest affair. At the outset – in 1888 – a golf course, several hotels, a beachside sanatorium, a pier and a large residential park had been planned, yet now, five years later, ambition would seem to be unmatched by financial resource. Furthermore, committee interference thwarts our gallant trio at every turn, and, although two hotels, a promenade and perhaps 30 houses have been completed, prospects for further progress are not good. In due course, Davies, Jones and Jones slip into obscurity.

Salem Chapel after an arson attack in 1913 Gwilym Jones

The accused. Gwilym Jones

But Mr Andrews, one suspects, is little interested in gloomy stories, and, certainly, committees hold no fascination for him. He is 58 years of age and has created, in his time, a business empire stretching from Cardiff to Liverpool and Manchester, from Plymouth to Belfast. In these places, fleets of omnibuses carry his name, while streets and properties bear his hallmark. Together with his son, Francis Emile, he is engaged in transport, furnishing, removals, confectionery. He owns a colliery and a string of coffee taverns. His vibrant office – a wing of the fabulously-

Victoria Parade, South Beach.
Wrench

ornate Cardiff Market – is known as Solomon's Temple. He inspires fierce loyalties and is unacquainted with self-doubt.

Solomon Andrews looks over the bay towards the mountains in the east. He looks along the shore past Carreg-y-Defaid, to the headland at Llanbedrog. He looks at the gold dusty sand beneath his feet, at the hills behind him and the virgin land between. He will make something of this!

And now he can see, perhaps, what others cannot even imagine: a hotel at least to equal South Beach, a terrace of lordly mansions, horse-drawn trams – toast racks and saloons – bobbing and jangling along a grand promenade. And – deep in the future, possibly beyond even his remarkable dreams – sweet-smiling bathing belles emerging from

The 'yellow brick road'.

West End, ancient and modern.

cheerful beach huts; rakish gents with silver-tipped canes and devil-may-care moustaches; gorgeous ladies with gossamer parasols; children, splashing and laughing, 'hiding-and-seeking'. He sees shining carriages and horses of pedigree; pierrots, fiddlers, actors, orchestras; tented stalls for shady refreshment. A theatre, church, post office, recreation ground; a freshly-greened golf course. Out at sea, dashing

West End Parade.

sails below the horizon and ferry boats skipping to the islands from the promenade pier. He will make a 'yellow brick road' called Cardiff, a bridge called Solomon, a tramway to the Maes, and he will call his resort West End.

But in truth you cannot imagine what he sees, for – like William Madocks – he is a man of unusual vision. And (again like Mr Madocks) he is a hard-headed businessman: decisive, competitive, confident of success, unafraid of failure. West End will be no South Beach!

As 1893 unfolds, Mr Andrews will enter a phase of tireless activity. He will establish a horse-drawn tramway to carry building stone from Carreg-y-Defaid (a quarry he will lease from the Love Jones Parrys of Madryn), two-and-a-half miles along the shore. He will complete the West End Hotel and promenade, and he will build an esplanade of stately terraced houses overlooking the bay. In the summer of 1894 an eager public will be allowed access to his tramway, which will soon be extended to the gates of Plas Glyn-y-Weddw – a Llanbedrog mansion he has purchased and converted into an art gallery. He will fight a serious medical battle, undergo the amputation of a leg, and yet he will remain undaunted. He will watch, helpless, as his tramway is devastated by an autumn storm. He will rebuild and re-route it across the dunes.

He will challenge officialdom, win his argument, and he will inaugurate a second tramway – from West End to the town centre – within a year.

And in 1897 – barely four years after his first, fateful visit – he will be awarded Pwllheli's ultimate honour, the freedom of the town.

In no time at all, West End and the 'Llanbedrog adventure' will be on everyone's calendar, and, as early as 1897, even the Cambrian Railway Company will join the growing chorus of approbation.

ALL VISITORS TO NORTH WALES SHOULD GO TO PWLLHELI
STAY AT THE WEST END HOTEL (84 rooms)
OR
AT ONE OF THE MANY LODGING HOUSES ON THE ESPLANADE...
And do not miss the invigorating, health-promoting tramway to
PLAS GLYN-Y-WEDDW

Few visitors can resist the 'quaint little cars', with their jovial little oil lamps, the breezy summer toast racks and the proximity of the sea – 'exciting and unusual'. Who would give a fig about sharp winds and bumpy rides? Even the frequent derailments are 'all part of the fun, it being the privilege of the Male Element to heave the trolley into the rails again!'

Moved, perhaps by Pwllheli's unconditional recognition, and inspired, no doubt, by the immediacy of his accomplishments, it becomes clear that what had begun purely as a business assignment

A toast rack to Llanbedrog. The wind in their hair!

Solomon Andrews.

is evolving into nothing less than a labour of love: a situation apparently confirmed by Mr Andrews's acquisition – as the family's summer residence – of No.12, the Promenade. At the same time his ambitions continue to soar and, although his pier project collapses, in the next few years he builds, together with 'Francis E', the Assembly Rooms for plays and concerts, the famous Recreation Ground with tennis courts and cycle track, the golf course and, in 1906, the Post Office.

Solomon Andrews dies in 1908, at least 15 years before his resort's finest hours. He will not know of his family's efforts to continue his work. He will not experience the railway-fired boom in tourism, nor will he be aware of West End's rising reputation as a health resort. He will not see the hot-air balloon sail over his promenade, and he will miss the flying display distinguished by the failure of Mr Astley's famous monoplane to clear the boundary wall! He will not see West End and South Beach joined together in 1915, and he will never know that the great National Eisteddfod of 1925 takes place on his very own Recreation Ground.

And, thankfully, he will not be aware that, in spite of everything, Pwllheli never actually does become a major seaside resort.

Promenade:
West End to Llanbedrog

Opposite: 'No.1', the tram to Llanbedrog.

We shall leave West End, as thousands have done before us, on Solomon Andrews' Llanbedrog tramway. Unfortunately, since the line was destroyed in 1927 and was never rebuilt, it will be a journey in the imagination. But that should not be too difficult on this wonderful shore.

PERSONS GETTING
OFF THESE CARS
WHILST IN MOTION DO
SO AT THEIR OWN RISK
1

The passing loop.

So, 'here we go! Leaving the Parade,
along the Promenade, and onto the
beach… the wind in our hair…
The long passing-loop at Tyddyn
Caled Farm, Carreg-y-Defaid still
in the distance… past the looters'
Gallows, Traeth Crugan and onward
'to Cae Fadog, where the
screech of brakes as we turn
the sharp bend tells us we are
100 yards from our destination.'

Alternatively, you may walk along the shore and scramble over Carreg-y-Defaid.

Carreg-y-Defaid.

The Mansion. Cath Hope

VIII Plas Glyn-y-Weddw, the Widow's Glen

It has been an exciting ride, over dune and shingle, a little tipsy perhaps on the loop, cutting in 'through luxuriant lanes…the land mingling with the sea.'

Coming to the gate and stepping down, you follow the path to the 'widow's fair stone-built mansion'. Through gardens steeped in

House and gardens, 'steeped in hyperbole'.

The Welsh Ladies Orchestra.
rhiw.com

hyperbole; blue skies peeping through tall, dark, handsome trees; glimpses of long Gothic windows behind the foliage; the sound of waves breaking on the shore below.

And of music: *Ramona*. Is this the Glyn Ladies Orchestra or the Bijou Orchestra? Your pace quickens to the rhythms of *Soldiers in the Park*, and slackens again as Miss Elsie Cookson begins to sing *One Fine Day*.

'Have you danced at Glyn Weddw?' everyone will ask. There are Dance Teas from four o'clock to six o'clock each day – at no extra charge. Or – for your special occasions – evening dances on Tuesdays and Fridays – tickets 5/-, including the return tram to West End.

You enter the gallery and look around: the breathtaking grand staircase and stained-glass window; the soaring beams and sunlit lantern... an ideal setting for Gainsborough, Landseer and Turner.

No wonder the widow's ghost lingers here, as if unable to tear itself away. Perhaps it even sleeps here – something, they say, the widow

The widow's gentlemen.
rhiw.com

Above left: 'A fair stone-built mansion'.
Above: The magnificent staircase and stained-glass window.

herself never managed to do. Not once in 25 years. And yet she would frequently visit this place, her dower house and gallery, driving down from Madryn in the family carriage.

What kind of person was this woman – this so-called 'miserly' widow – Lady Elizabeth Love Jones Parry, who would carefully measure every penny, yet would spend £20,000 on her beloved house and garden? What would she demand of Henry Kennedy, the mansion's architect? How would she behave towards him and towards others? How would she regard her servants? With whom would she share confidences? Would she lay flowers at St Pedrog, beside her husband's grave, and how would she regard her wayward son's feverish exploits? And when, in 1883, Lady Elizabeth passed away and became ghostly, would she have been – as was one of her ancient forebears – 'universally lamented because universally loved'? Or would her demise have been a matter of little import?

After the widow's death the mansion was leased to the Angersteins, a Russian banking and art-loving family with Tsarist connections; and then, in 1896 – an opportune moment indeed for Solomon Andrews – the property appeared as LOT 1 in the sale of the 'outlying portions of Madryn Park Estate':

> ...situate in what may be termed
> The Cambrian Riviera. Grounds
> well-studded with fine specimens
> of timber trees and shrubs...

enhanced by the bold rockwork
of Mynydd Tir-y-Cwmwd.

Mr Andrews must have rubbed his hands together: house and 196 acres, his for £7,000.

In the 1970s Plas Glyn-y-Weddw began another phase in its distinguished career. Purchased by the artist Gwyneth ap Tomos and husband Dafydd, the mansion was patiently restored and made once again into a fine gallery and arts centre. Surely neither mansion nor gardens could ever have been more impressive than they are today. And incidentally, looking out over the gardens to the sea, the conservatory tearoom is a sheer delight.

As you leave the widow's garden you will see the church of St Pedrog on your left. Though the present building dates from 1865, the church's foundation reaches back to the sixth century.

St Pedrog's was particularly badly treated during the Civil War when requisitioned as Cromwellian stables. Walls, windows and graves were mutilated or destroyed, and it was Cromwell's commander-on-the-spot, Geoffery Parry, who was the man responsible. At which point history decrees a twist! Geoffery Parry – Puritan to the bone – meets and falls in love with a young Royalist lady from Wern Fawr. Putting politics to one side they marry and have a son. They call him, somewhat bizarrely, Love God Parry. The son dispenses with 'God' and is known simply as Love. It is Love who atones for his father's misdeeds, restores the church and becomes its generous benefactor. Love, it must be, who is 'universally lamented', and it is for Love that villagers deck 'the hedges… between Wern Fawr and St Pedrog… with black flannel on the day of his funeral'.[14]

Memorial stone to Sir Thomas Duncombe Jones Parry, Bart.

And later, much later, a certain Love Jones Parry of Madryn will meet the lady Elizabeth; and it is she who will become the widow of our story.

Elizabeth's son, Thomas Love Duncombe, will be wayward and hedonistic. Facing execution in Spain, he will be set free only after the intercession of Queen Victoria; he will help – in some obscure way – to establish the Welsh colony in Patagonia; and, in 1868, he will become the Liberal MP for Caernarfon.

It is said that Sir Thomas Love Duncome Jones Parry,

A Llanbedrog wedding conducted by Mr Maley in 1920.

Anne and Henry Roberts

Bart, only ever asked one parliamentary question: could someone please open a window?

Coming down to Llanbedrog beach from Plas Glyn-y-Weddw is – to coin a phrase – like stepping into a beautiful picture: all honey-gold, slate-grey, sepia. A colour splash of bathing huts all in a row, red, blue, green, yellow, a distant promontory of amber stone, a cottage or two, hiding in the shadows. Trees overstep the sand, the sea is smooth and silvery.

And, what is more, you can enjoy paella and a sherry trifle here on the delightful terrace at Y Gali, or relax with a beer.

However… we ought really to move on.

Beach huts, Llanbedrog.

Peter Leslie

A coal ship unloads.
Gwilym Jones

Promenade:
Llanbedrog to Abersoch

Our next destination, Abersoch, is two miles beyond Mynydd Tir-y-Cwmwd, Llandbedrog's defining mountain. You may choose from several routes, the first of which takes you over the mountain itself.

The steep, rugged steps that climb Mynydd Tir-y-Cwmwd begin beside the boathouse at the end of the beach. It is not the easiest of ascents, but it is at least brief and, as you might expect, the visual rewards are generous. At the top, an Iron Man stands and stares, the wind whistling through his bones.[15] Good paths cut through the gorse

Llanbedrog beach, looking towards Carreg-y-Defaid

Opposite: Traeth Ty'n Tywyn. The skeletal remains of a miners' jetty.

and heather, encircle or cross the plateau, rise to the summit or follow the cliffs. Eventually, you can meet the old lane from Llanbedrog. Turn left at the junction and left again after the cottage called 'Geufron', and you will soon come to the beach.

If, however, you have no appetite for the climb, you may – at low tide – scramble round the base of the headland. It is a poignant scene, revealing, as it does, many a reminder of the mountain's working past: abandoned ochre-rock quarries, deserted sills and half-cut stone faces, and, as you come to the broader sands, the withered timber legs – skeletal remains of a miners' jetty.

Should neither climbing nor scrambling appeal, however, a third route, easier by far, is readily available. Craig y Llan, the old lane from Llanbedrog, skirts the highest ground and converges with the upland path a short distance before 'Geufron'. The lane itself begins beside what was once St Pedrog's church hall, a building today housing the village's Knitting and Sewing Guild.

Aim now for Penbennar and the jetty at Abersoch, two glorious miles away: offshore, the vast safe haven known as St Tudwal's Road, and to the south-west, the self-same saint's islands, Ynysoedd Tudwal. Walk along Traeth Ty'n Tywyn, pass the Warren, the high dunes and the low, pitted cliffs – in Norman times, the site of a castle. If the tide is out, the Afon Soch will not delay you. However, you may prefer to leave the beach at the lifeboat station, join the main road at 'Land and Sea' and cross the bridge into the village.

At high tide you will not be able to pass the low cliffs, in which case you should leave the beach at the Warren's launching post.

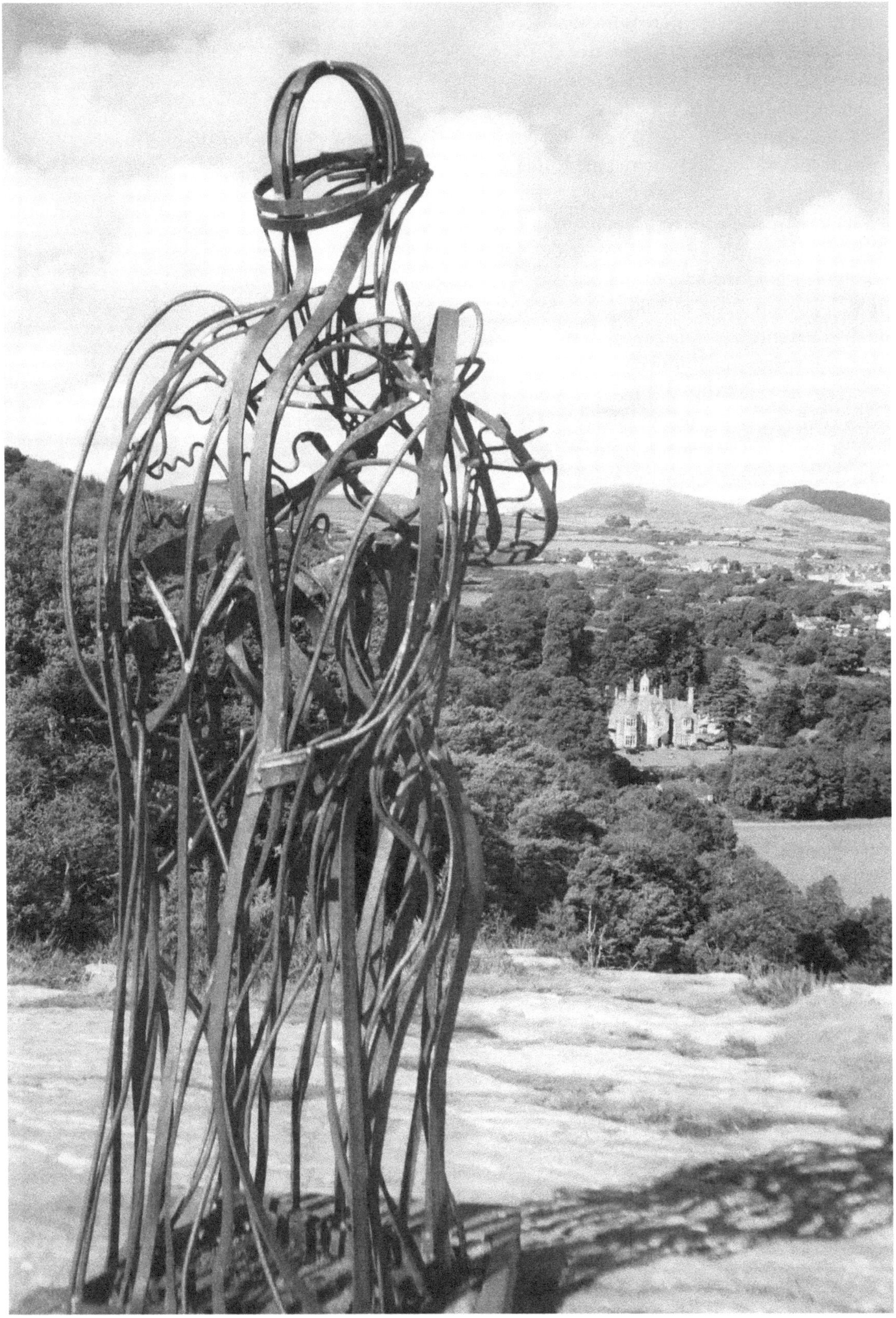

IX Abersoch

Opposite: The iron man looking towards Plas Glyn-y-Weddw.

The season will define Abersoch's greeting. Summer is over. Away with wakeboards and wetsuits; with saltfish, ackees and pumpkin soup; with Oxbow pink bikinis and Fat Face squidgy flops. Disarm the powerboat, muzzle the jetski, fold the sails and mothball the chalet. Forget Gosling's Meals on Keels and 5° West. Delete all references to tequilas and chillis and hot bananas in chocolate sauce. Dispense with the smoothies and breezers. Stack the tables and sunshades, silence the Sandpiper and save Mañana for another day... blessed relief (or, alternatively, unreserved tedium) is just around the corner!

It has been a momentous summer: a season to corroborate Abersoch's long tradition of 'keeping visitors'. Beginning in June – with stallions and jazz bands, and grey-headed ladies jigging through the streets with colourful rococo brollies – it has seemed to last forever.

The old harbour at Abersoch.

TRACY-LOUISE
MH53

GEMINI

The harbour in days gone by.

Wave upon wave of holidaymakers arriving in a spin – the Brightwells, the Winterbottoms and the Chadwicks. The good, the bad and the beautiful. A few – but just a few – with the Big City still on their breath, unable to shed their urban impatience and failing to see that such things do not impress anyone here. Others, gentler perhaps, a little bewildered, with three infants, a puppy and high hopes. In the village, cafés and pubs are seething; lanes clogged with cars; enormous boats and unwieldy caravans squeezing through the narrow streets and struggling round the corner at Talafon.

Here are the golden-shouldered young – sexily midriffed, handsomely six-packed, minimally attired – browsing at Rip Girl, hanging around The Vaynol; strutting, being seen, striking attitudes; revving up hi-profile, hi-decibel engines on land and sea; tracking the beat. Over here, a swagger of townies affecting ennui, there, a pride of surfers 'tearing up fresh powder... harnessing a wave'.

And the elders, scorching down from Sarn Bach for a take-away, or sweeping in from their dune-side villas for hazelnut latte at the Yacht Club. Craving brill and crayfish Florentine, desperate to reserve a table at Tremfan or Plas Bodegroes. Or mooching around priceless beach huts, discussing the tidal factors in driving their boats over to Shell Island.

The less grandiose – looking distinctly pink – digging channels and moats, hurling frisbees or just taking it easy. Swarms of children, swathed in suncream, hooting and squealing. Demanding crisps from Footprints.

Captain Harry Parry, bearded, with a group of Abersoch mariners. Captain Parry lived on his ship, which he would draw up the beach above high water.

rhiw.com

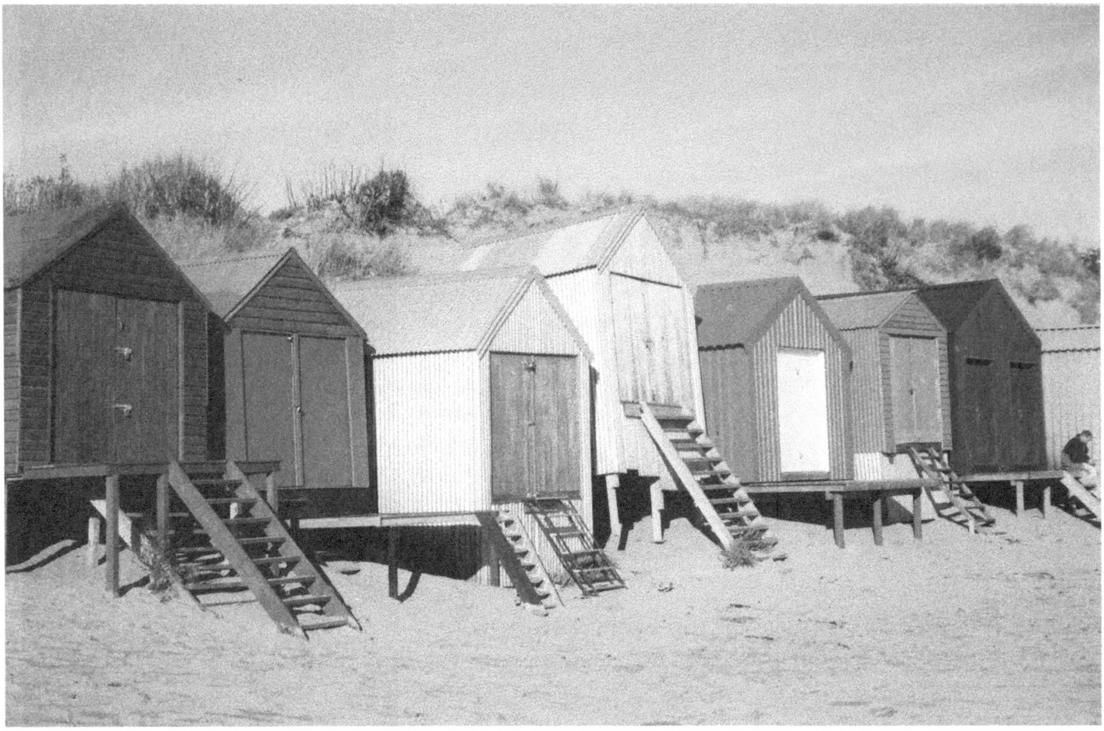

Desirable, but painfully expensive, beach huts.

Yes, it has been a long, noisy, fun-packed season of regattas and competitions, flag days and exhibitions. From Jazz Band Ball to the Laser Nationals, from the tumultuous Wakestock and the Great Raft Race, to Pandora, Sonata and Squib. From Tidal Aid to October Surf, this was Abersoch's summer greeting: something – as they say – for everyone.

Opposite: The beach at Machroes.

End of season.

Unless, of course, you are set upon quiet contemplation! In which case, Abersoch's fortissimo season is best avoided. But be patient. Let the days dwindle, and, as autumn creeps in across the sea – the colours turn and the air becomes clear with the cold – it will bring with it a gradual diminuendo, settling finally into winter's faultless lente... time to rest, time to think.

Or, time to rediscover Abersoch's other life: residents emerging from summer hibernation, reclaiming the streets, re-activating schools, and, some of them, re-establishing, as best they can, the neglected cadences of Cymraeg.

Or, time to walk with ghosts! Just look at those pale picture-postcard cottages and those elevated white villas facing each other across forsaken streets – vacant-eyed, dust-sheeted, drained. See the shuttered cafés, disowned shops and beer-less beer gardens; the shelves of untended caravans gazing blankly across the bay. Look at the piled-high bathing hutches at Penbennar, climbing above the shore, with the haunted look of a hastily-abandoned desert encampment. It is often written that in winter Abersoch feels like a ghost town, and, while this is by no means true of the village centre, the outer reaches do indeed appear possessed of a ghostly quality.

Old Abersoch. rhiw.com

Perhaps this is the inevitable price to be paid by a community obedient to the holidaymaker,

Afon Soch, low tide.
Gwilym Jones

a seasonal paradise 'hinged on beach culture'. It is what Elfed Gruffydd describes (with admirable restraint) as a 'prime example of the two cultures' – on the one hand, a teeming summer resort, on the other, a quiet winter village.[16]

Yet, for all this, winter may be the best of all seasons to take to the beach; to walk along Borth Fawr and Traeth Machroes towards the old lifeboat house at Penrhyn Du; to allow your mind to play over the landscape. See how the bays to the north lead the eye to Mynydd Tir-y-Cwmwd, and how Penbennar – their centrepoint – appears to be positioned with meticulous care. It is no accident that this area has earned the coveted status of Outstanding Natural Beauty; it is no coincidence that the Heritage Coast begins here.

You may have concluded from all this talk of high jinks, holidays and pretty views that Abersoch is somehow devoid of any real historical

Morning delivery, Talafon.
rhiw.com

interest. But, you would have been quite wrong. Yes, it is true that even at the beginning of the 19th century there was little more here than 'a few houses upon the edge of St Tudwal's Road'. But this tells us almost nothing about an ancient place shaped by kings, sages and warriors, a place in which fact and fable have often united both to illuminate and to deceive.

Did you know, for instance, that in days of yore, a troupe of fairies would quite regularly visit Felin Soch to borrow pans in which to bake their bread? And that – having done so – they would leave a little loaf as a thank-you gift for the woman at the mill? Sneer if you like, but do so with caution, for in the woods above the mill fairy rings can be seen to this day.

'Castellmarch'.

The house called 'Castellmarch' sits innocuously beside the road from Llanbedrog for all to see. But did you know that a former building on the site was occupied by March ap Meirchion, a knight at King Arthur's table – a personage, furthermore, with horse's ears? And did you know that one day, no longer able to contain his painful secret, he rode down to the river and confided in the reeds; that the reeds – clearly undeserving of his confidence – informed a passing musician; and that when the musician played his pipe, the secret floated out for all to hear?

The existence of Sarn Badrig – St Patrick's Causeway – reaching out beneath the sea towards Harlech, cannot be denied. But did you know that the Causeway was once an embankment bordering the magic kingdom of Cantre'r Gwaelod – a land inundated by the sea when its bibulous watchman inadvertently left open the gate? You may doubt it, but do so guardedly, for one day you may hear the bells of Cantre'r Gwaelod chiming under the water.[17]

History. Who could resist it!

Beyond the old lifeboat house at Penrhyn Du you may be able to clamber over the rocks to Porth Bach: a place of instantaneous seclusion, soothing and exhilarating in equal measure and a powerful catalyst to even a modest imagination. See the endless waves roll and break. These are the very waves that once took 15 ships in a single night. See the spray lifting and hanging suspended over St Tudwall's eastern isle, and imagine the exertions and torments of the men who built its saintly priory. Sing the song of *Fflat Huw Puw*, and picture the old ship labouring towards Llanbedrog Head and certain disaster. Here, too, secreted within the rocky mass behind you, are the long-renounced lead mines of Penrhyn Du. Many say the Romans worked these mines. But who knows?

Above: The song of Fflat Huw Puw.

Eunice Jones

Above left: J. Glynne Davis (driving the cart), composer of the song.

rhiw.com

The cliffs beyond Porth Bach – increasingly aggressive – will bar the way to all but the adventurer, and so (unless rock climbing is among your specialities) you would be well advised to return to Traeth Machroes and walk up the hill towards the houses.[18]

Now, where the lanes cross, the Llŷn will offer you a welter of options, among them Porth Ceiriad and Mynydd Cilan, neither of which should be missed. Hear the sounds of the sea echoing around Ceiriad's spectacular amphitheatre; gaze in awe upon the cliffs of Pared Mawr; stand atop Mynydd Cilan and look towards Porth Neigwl and Mynydd y Graig.

Should you wish, you may now head back to the shore. If so, aim for Nant Farm and the footpath to Porth Neigwl. In two hours – seas, gods and landslips willing – you will be climbing the stairway, if not to paradise then at least to Rhiw.

Alternatively, take the overland route to Llanengan and Llangian, villages associated with the Bardsey pilgrims, and visit their churches –

Rhuol, part of Rhiw.

rhiw.com

St Cian's Church, Llangian.

The Tanrallt lead mine, Llanengan.

St Engan and St Cian: churches 'blessed with comfort', it has been said! See the magnificent carved rood screen at St Engan, and – in the churchyard of St Cian – the fifth or sixth-century memorial stone dedicated to *Melus Medici, Fili Martini* – Melus the doctor, Son of Martinus. A treasure indeed!

A Family Album

Henry and Anne Roberts

Recollections of Llŷn...

Of the children of Siop Tŷ Newydd at Hell's Mouth,

Griffith Owen Jones on the left...

of Griffith Owen's wedding...

of a wedding in Llannor in the 1920s...

of 'Trefaes Bella' farm…

harvesting,

carrying,

threshing,

of the new tractor…

Of schools and outings

Standards 3,4 and 5, Sarn Meyllteyrn Primary School. This small school was one of the first to be affected by the 1960s closures in North Wales.

Ysgol Botwnnog senior football team, 1965–66.

of the school garden at Sarn,

Of the people who moved away…

to nursing duties in Bournville,

to the coalfields of South Wales,

to Canada with her soldier,

to the 'silver rush' in Denver…

And of those who stayed…

Great grandfather, Harry and great grandmother, Dora,

Griffith Jones of 'Cae'r Llo', great great great grandfather,

Griffith Roberts of 'Nant Selar', great great grandfather,

Grandfather William

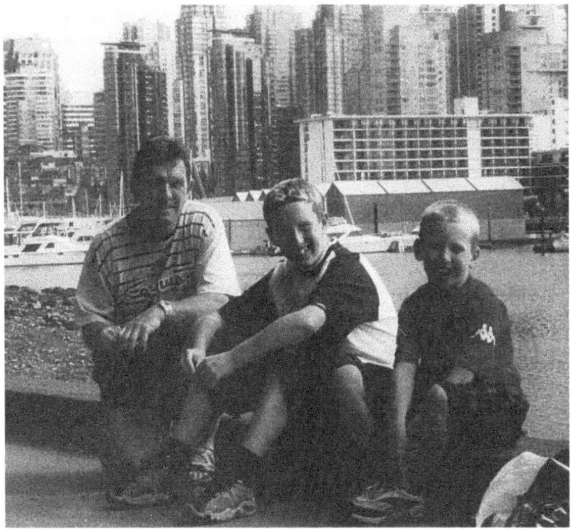

Father, Henry, and sons Osian and Steffan.

Dear Motorist

If you have driven from the Madogs to Abersoch, for much of the journey you will have enjoyed the favours of a splendid highway.

Coming out of Porthmadog – skirting the austere northern face of Moel-y-Gest and the milder slopes of Moel-y-Gadair – you will soon have swept towards the coast, and you may have paused at the lookout high above Cricieth to see the bay and the castle. Staying on the main road, you will have bypassed Lloyd George's Village, and you may have allowed Penarth Fawr – an exquisite mediaeval house – to slip by unnoticed. You may also have missed – at Abererch – the ancient church of St Cawrdraf.

Yet, you will have arrived at Pwllheli light of heart, for chances are you had never expected a road such as this! Although – picking your way through the busy streets of Llŷn's capital – you may have faltered, your spirits will have been restored as you continued towards Llanbedrog.

You will have ignored the turn-off to Efailnewydd, disregarded the Polish Village – not to mention the giant's graveyard – at Penrhos and dismissed the spur to Plas Glyn-y-Weddw. Dropping down to Abersoch harbour you will have reached the village in rude excitement. How, in anticipation, you had misjudged the roads of Penrhyn Llŷn!

At which point something quite extraordinary happens: this excellent road you have for so long pursued, admired and trusted, climbs the hill, encircles the upper village, and, without a word of explanation, heads back to Pwllheli! It simply deserts you.

But fear not! There is a world beyond Abersoch. Indeed, there are two: one in which the rituals of summer persist, and another – quite different – a world more traditional, in which the concept of remoteness gathers substance; where some families have lived for generations and wouldn't move if you paid them; where roads quickly diminish into lanes, and lanes become narrow tracks that creep between high hedges, cling to hillsides, squeeze across tiny bridges, clatter over cattle grids and sneak into farmyards. These are the byways where hay wagons loom, sheep stray, and where tractors are the vehicles of privilege.

So, my dear motorist, be warned! If you venture into these parts, go softly. And if you are by nature a king of the road who equates deference with defeat, it may be best if you don't go at all!

A vehicle of privilege.
Cath Hope

THE PROVERBIAL SLATE

by Henry Roberts

Llŷn, like most rural areas, was serviced by a number of small, often remote, family-run shops selling a wide range of goods. These shops were usually a room in a house or a nearby outbuilding. The number of small shops declined regularly from the 1930s onwards, though some were still trading in the early 1970s.

An old account book.

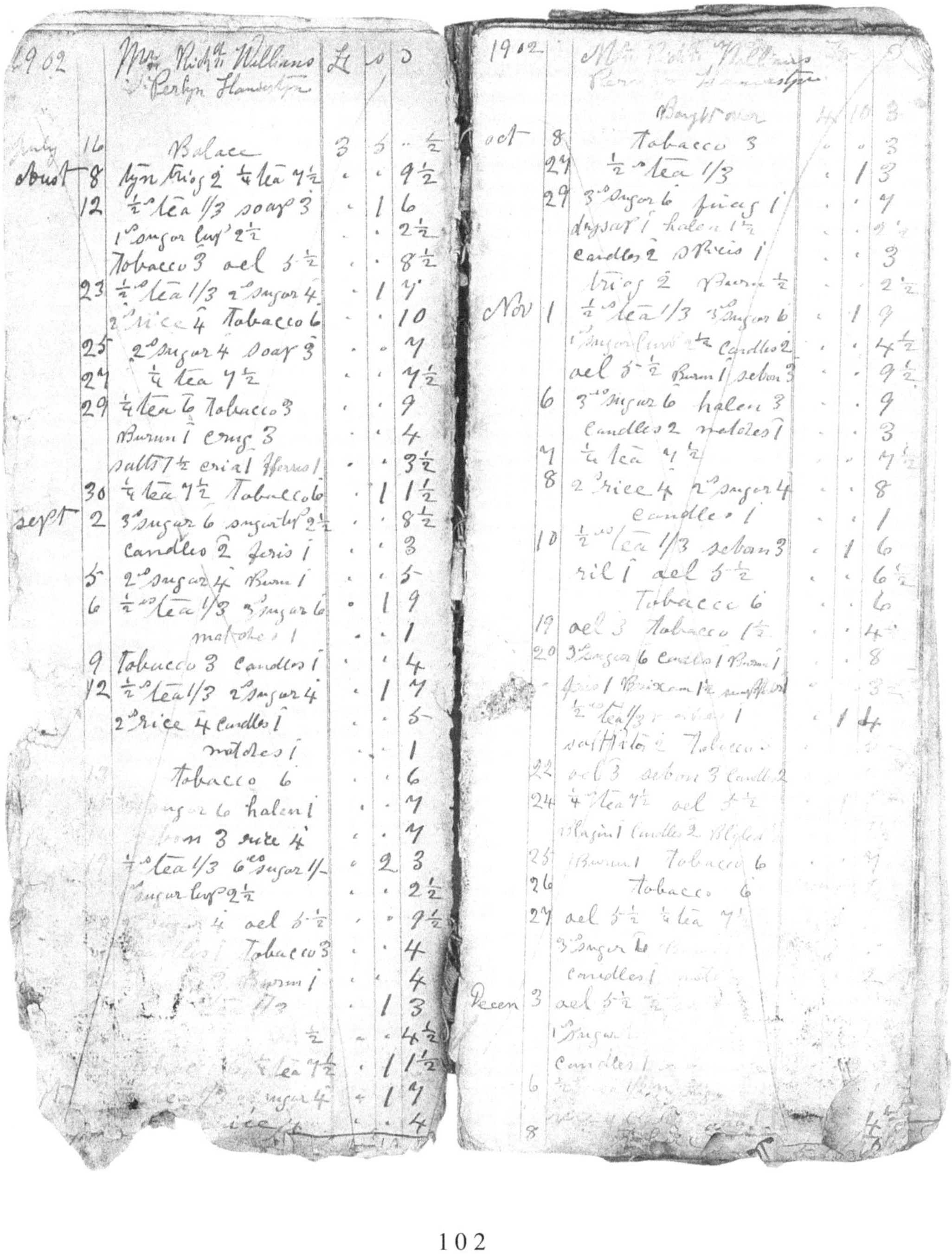

One such shop was run at Trefaes Bach, a small mud-walled house located close to the centre of a deep rural triangle formed by the villages of Botwnnog, Llaniestyn and Sarn Meyllteyrn. A tattered account book (the proverbial 'slate') from this shop has recently been discovered covering the period between 1899 and the last entry in 1925, and a copy of part of this account book is reproduced here. Though at first glance it is merely a list of items with prices alongside, it speaks volumes about life in rural Llŷn during the period leading up to and including World War One.

The picture created is of a community well educated in the 'three Rs' in both languages, and buying a wide range of basic goods, including tea, coffee, biscuits, mustard, sauce, and others such as candle and lamp oil – necessities of that period. People travelled (mostly on foot) well over a mile for their shopping (one family over three miles), though this trend might be exaggerated in the account book by family and other ties, and the obvious availability of credit.

Life would have been hard during this time and some customers inevitably had difficulties with their repayments. Some debts seem not to have been honoured, others are shown to have been repaid in kind. One tailor settles his account by making a 'top coat' for the shop owner, a blacksmith carries out work in his forge, a farmer brings eggs from his farm, and someone called 'Evan' repays with his labour. Some customers actually borrowed money from the shop. The blacksmith is an interesting example. He lived some distance from the shop. From 1898 to September 1905 all seemed to be well. However, by the end of 1906 he had run up a debt of £25 11s 10d, a sum equivalent to £700 by today's valuation. This was partly repaid by 'work in the smith' – 'gwaith yn yr efail' to the sum of £17 1s 2d in February 1907. The blacksmith made only one purchase thereafter, but borrowed a total of £15 0s 0d (today's valuation about £450) between then and 1925! The total of £23 12s 10d still had not been crossed from the accounts in April 1925 and is the last entry made.

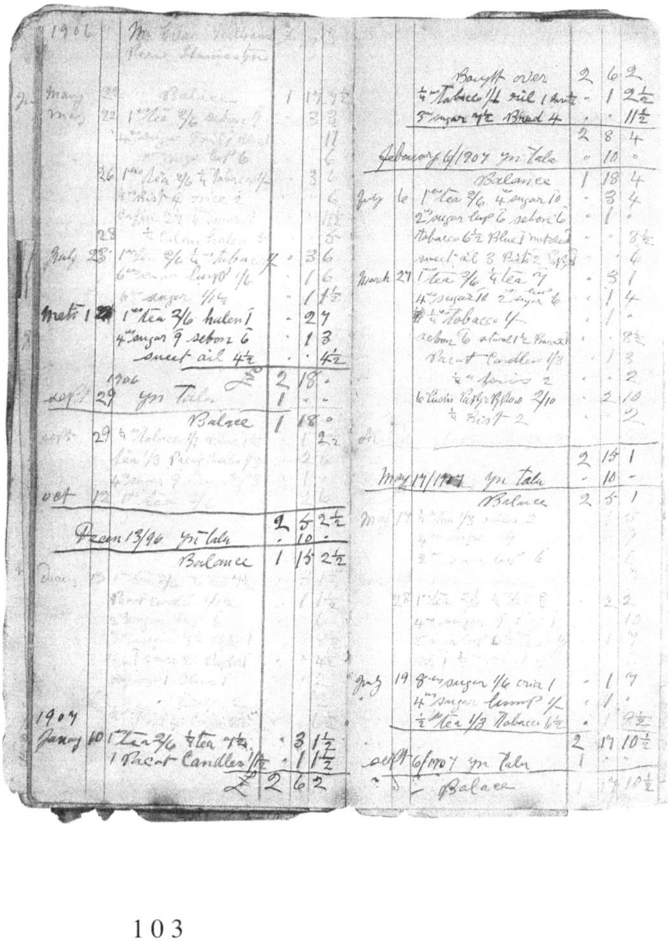

X Plas yn Rhiw

The open, wind-stripped hills of the southern shores bear witness to violent winters. Rocks are bare, trees stooped, vegetation tough, resilient, furtive. Yet even here, in the more sheltered valleys and on the sunnier slopes, small oases of almost Mediterranean lushness can be found. In one such corner, overlooking Hell's Mouth and secreted deep in woodland a mile or two east of the village of Rhiw, is the lovely old house called Plas yn Rhiw. It was in this house that the Keating women lived.

Plas yn Rhiw. rhiw.com

The story of the acquisition, in 1938, and subsequent restoration of what had been at the time an abandoned country estate has been painstakingly documented. How the Keating sisters from Nottingham – Eileen, Lorna and Honora – together with their widowed mother Constance, had fallen under Llŷn's spell while on family holidays and had longed to settle here; how the absentee owner of Plas yn Rhiw, a house of ancient foundation, had somehow been located, and how negotiations for its purchase had been concluded. Although Honora had continued to pursue her career in child welfare in the south of England, the sisters had proceeded to devote much of their time to the rebuilding of the house, the restoration of the gardens, and the restitution of the estate's scattered domains. It is told how Clough Williams-Ellis, family friend and creator of Portmeirion, had helped them realise their vision and how, little by little, house and garden had become a place of singular beauty.

Eileen, Lorna and Honora Keating in the garden, 1960. rhiw.com

So much, and much more is recorded. But what cannot easily be captured are those particular qualities that make Plas yn Rhiw so special. It is not a great and illustrious house. Not a swaggering architectural spectacle or a noble palace where gilt-framed seraphs and

The hall, as restored by Clough Williams-Ellis. rhiw.com

graces cavort in long galleries, or where gleaming tables are set for 100 glittering guests; not a place where suits of armour peer from every dark corner. Nor are its gardens wonders of complex geometrics with mazes, fountains, cascades, and with follies and shooting towers so distant as to be barely visible.

Plas yn Rhiw is special because it is so clearly at ease with itself and with its natural surroundings. And because in contrast to the Georgian poise and moderation of its exterior, inside it manages to catch – with the help of a Gothic doorway here, a hidden staircase or an archway there – something of its architect's eccentric magic.

But just as telling are the objects and articles which transform the house from historical specimen into living organism: paintings and drawings – many of them by Honora (a graduate of London's Slade School of Art) and by her friends – of Constance, Aunt Emma, baby William, of Mynydd Rhiw and Porth Neigwl; sketch pads and postcards; a wind-up gramophone with 'The Laughing Policeman' ready for duty; Aladdin wicks, a vintage teasmade and trusty typewriter. There are books: collections by Goethe and Shakespeare neatly counter-balanced by *Three Bright Girls* and *Français pour les Jeunes*; the poems of R.S. Thomas (who, incidentally, in his retirement lived in a cottage on the estate), and recollections of Rhiw by Sir Compton Mackenzie (one of the family's celebrated acquaintances). In the study, Honora's OBE citation (in recognition of her social work), and in the hall, a letter from Clough Williams-Ellis.

And everywhere, a digest of the grand and the ordinary: precious Viennese vases and two-a-penny pot basins; a refined 18th-century games table, a rugged, no-nonsense Welsh cupboard; a rack of shoes; a Victorian patchwork quilt, Japanese woodcuts and stockings hung up to dry. And, on the kitchen table, a breakfast tray set for Eileen, complete with her morning post.

A quiet corner of Plas yn Rhiw.

In the garden, too, a disarming mixture of the exotic and the familiar. Secret retreats and winding paths, formal rectangles of box hedging; a little stone cottage, and a sheltered terrace with rickety wooden table, basket chairs and potted plants; a cobbled yard and a tiny waterfall; magnolia, fuchsia, azalea, camellia; steep wooded slopes and glimpses of the magnificent bay and the mountains beyond.

The Keating sisters were passionate conservationists who earned fearsome reputations for the intensity of their commitment. As the years went by they donated not only their beloved Plas yn Rhiw, but cottages, coves and mountains to the National Trust of Wales for safekeeping. And so, should you ever ramble across the heights of Mynydd Rhiw or Mynydd y Graig, or scramble down the cliffs and onto the beach at Porth Ysgo, it might be worth remembering that you are free to do so largely thanks to them.

A carpet of snowdrops.

HELL'S MOUTH AND *THE TWELVE APOSTLES*

Hell's Mouth. rhiw.com

Before we forsake the wooded gardens of Plas yn Rhiw – the great crescent of Hell's Mouth below us – we shall briefly revisit Henry Hughes, who, in *Immortal Sails*, tells the fascinating story of *The Twelve Apostles.*

It is a dark and stormy night in 1898. A gale-force wind and blinding rain. Heavy seas are sweeping along *The Twelve Apostles* in wild, uncontrolled rushes… making steering impossible.

Through the mist Captain Jones of Borth-y-Gest recognises a familiar mountain. It is Mynydd Rhiw! The schooner is trapped in the jaws of Hell's Mouth, the grave of many ships. The captain, realising the impossibility of escape, plays a last desperate card. He attempts to shape a course through the breakers and run the stricken schooner aground. But the fates are against him. A sudden violent impact seems to lift *The Twelve Apostles* from the sea… her masts rattle, her timbers grate as she falls on her wounded side, a helpless wreck.

Great waves begin their remorseless pounding and, as the crew

The Twelve Apostles. rhiw.com

struggle to launch their only boat, avalanches of sea tumble about them in a terrifying manner. Yet now, the ship settles, she forms a breakwater and at last the boat can be launched. A servant girl watching from the cliffs rushes down to the beach. She wades into the surf and steadies the boat as it reaches the shallows.

The Twelve Apostles is consumed, but not a single life is lost.

The church at Llanfaelrhys.
rhiw.com

Around Rhiw

A little beyond Mynydd Rhiw, towards Llanfaelrhys and between the cliffs of Môr and the crags of Penarfynydd, is a tiny church.

It is silent here since the church, dedicated to St Maelrhys, lies in open countryside some distance from the road through Rhiw. It is a building of childlike simplicity unadorned by decoration. Inside, the combination of white walls, black box pews and plain benches is most striking. In this somewhat austere setting you may soon believe you have seen all there is to see. But don't rush away.

Stand before the altar and notice how the east window seems to draw in Mynydd Rhiw, Mynydd Graig and their scattered cottages. Framed in the sunrise arch of the window is a timeless, quite motionless picture: a stillness only your imagination can activate. It is an extinction to be challenged. So do it, and history once again will stir.

See some 20 hunters and gatherers returning at twilight to their encampment on the brown rocks; Roman soldiers dipping and dyeing robes and banners, using ore taken from beneath the very ground upon which they stand. Observe the fearsome princes and tribesmen of Rhiw: Meirion Goch, defender of the shores against Norse invaders, and his son, Cynyllion the Horseman; the chieftain Heili galloping wildly towards Cadlan and his kinsmen, Einion and Bleddyn. Watch two robbers hurry from the church of St Maelrhys, bags bulging with silver, and marvel as – before your very eyes – they are petrified in punishment for their crime. Look how they are transformed into mere sculptures of men, and see how sorry they look. Watch out for John ap Lewis ap Dafydd, racing towards his estate at Plas yn Rhiw. Witness the arrest of Morgan y Gogrwr, Methodist fanatic. Note his ineffective attempt to elicit mercy by parading his two children before the court, and – as he is despatched across the sea – be mindful of the futility of emotional blackmail in the presence of a scrupulous judge. Hear the tappings and scrapings from the axe factory on the slopes of Rhiw; the whispered prayers of the Bardsey pilgrims; the grumbling of, oh, 200 men as they to-and-fro around the busy manganese mines. And watch the women rinsing the mineral before directing it, via pulleys and trolleys, to the boats moored at the jetties of Ysgo and Neigwl.

What a fertile imagination you have! And one with scant regard, it seems, for detail and chronology. But, no matter. For the time being savour the excitement. Soon enough your books will restore order, and history will become, once again, a sentence on a page.

The churchyard of St Maelrhys – more extensive than might have been expected – is an open, treeless, shelter-less rectangle. Wander between the headstones and read the names and inscriptions carved upon them – sea captains, farmers, kindly mothers, healers, despots,

The churchyard of St Aelrhiw, idyllic in all respects but one: adders nesting in the grass!

heroes. Recite the names and the effect is almost hypnotic:

Mary Evans
John Evans Elizabeth Evans Griffith Evans
Owen Griffith John Griffith Griffith Griffiths
Jane Jones
James Jones Emrys Jones Gwilym Jones
Thomas Jones
Thomas Jones Thomas Jones Thomas Jones

A minimalist lyric. A genealogist's nightmare!

And then, beside the wall next to the lane, you will come across four names of a different ilk. Constance, Eileen, Lorna and Honora Keating. Mother and daughters in two simple graves: Constance Keating, 1860–1945, lying alone; and together at her feet, beneath a single rough slate slab, her daughters 'lifting up their eyes to the hills'.

Promenade: Rhiw to Aberdaron

Should you take the lane west from Rhiw, passing Llanfaelrhys on your left, you will see nothing of the coves and islands that lie behind the intervening slopes. But, by way of compensation, you will at least enjoy a splendid approach to Aberdaron. The village appears soon after you have passed 'Bryn Hywyn' on your right and although it is dangerous to stop at this point – the lane is narrow, the gradient steep – it is a prospect not to be disregarded.

But it is far better to walk from Rhiw to Aberdaron across the fields and cliffs which so handsomely link them. A plethora of footpaths allows you to choose your route, pace and preference, whether that be for ancient history, remnants of an industrial kind, or, perhaps, images of the unexpected – Cadlan, King Arthur's last battlefield; Gwenonwy, the king's sister, turned to stone and standing, forlorn, in the breaking waves. Or perhaps you would prefer simply to absorb the atmosphere of a place where every twist and turn reveals a new treasure – the distant stripes of Cilan, the Ysgo waterfall, or the Gwylans, Fawr and Bach.

Clough Williams-Ellis's Post Office, Aberdaron.

Cath Hope

XI Aberdaron

The quintessential seaside village should nestle in a hollow, half-surrounded by hills and headlands. It should feature a lovely old church overlooking the sea and – a few steps away – a couple of inns, one of which should be called The Ship. A winding stream, making its way to the shore, should pass huddles of white cottages and little shops. Yet the village should also claim a colourful history: fantastic wrecks and formidable rescues; desperate battles against remorseless seas; poets, sages and saints moderating the violent excesses of pirates, looters and wreckers.

Aberdaron – once described by an Irish traveller as a village 'transferred bodily from the operatic stage' – comfortably meets the varied demands of quintessence. It is at once resort and community, proud and hospitable, remote and comely.

Flanked by two promontories, the greater to the west, the lesser to the east, Aberdaron lies towards the end of a sandy bay. Her church does indeed overlook the sea and, sure enough, close by, two venerable inns – Tŷ Newydd and The Ship – eye each other, a little warily perhaps, across the street: Tŷ Newydd, defiantly prominent and happy to meet the wildest storms in order to boast 'breathtaking sea views', The Ship, cosier and more sheltered from the elements' worst excesses. A handful of shops – seasonal and otherwise – offer newspapers, provisions and seaside paraphernalia,

Tea party at Aberdaron.

rhiw.com

The village from above St Hywyn's Church.

while the inviting smell of warm crusty cobs wafts down the hill from Becwys Isllyn, the village bakery.

Today, you are lucky. It is a flawless July afternoon of crystal clarity, the sky unreasonably blue, a southern breeze easing the sun's intemperance. The shore no longer frequented by the piratical sons of Beelzebub but by families, becalmed, slowly grilling in the sunshine. The deadly rifles and sabres of yesterday's invaders, ousted by childish laser guns and yellow water pistols; the screams of storm-tossed mariners by bathers' laughter; illicit brandy and cheeses by fizzy drinks and sticky lollies.

Ty Newydd.

Pilgrims' delight – Y Gegin Fawr.

But of course there is much more to Aberdaron than meets the eye. Let us look back, far back. Fifteen hundred years or so.

It is the sixth century, and Gwyndaf Hen, together with the saintly Cadfan and a company of monks, has journeyed from Brittany to Llŷn's farthest shore. They will cross the treacherous waters to Bardsey Island, Ynys Enlli, where Cadfan will establish a monastery. As time goes by, this foundation will become so revered, that three visits to Enlli will be equal in sanctity to a pilgrimage to Rome and '20,000 saints' will be buried in the island's holy soil. Pilgrims will come from far and near, and the coastal tracks of Llŷn will be punctuated by places of worship and refreshment for those who make the journey.

The kitchen.

rhiw.com

Though not everyone will survive, the pilgrims who do reach Aberdaron will be fed at Y Gegin Fawr – the Big Kitchen – and will give thanks at the church on the shore, a church dedicated to St Hywyn, son of that ancient traveller, Gwyndaf Hen, and Confessor to Cadfan himself.

The church of St Hywyn seems to emanate from the sand upon which it rests, its western gables – one squatter and older than its partner – creating the perfect equilibrium between unequal elements, its posture denying an unsettled history of service, decay, abandonment and recovery.

Traffic jam! rhiw.com

Established in the darkest of ages (though the present building dates from the 12th to the 16th century), St Hywyn's – the so-called 'cathedral of Llŷn' – has befriended pilgrim, pauper, prince and monarch. For centuries, within these walls the meek have been fortified, the hasty placated, the thoughtful provoked. Indeed, in quite recent times, the great Welsh poet, R.S. Thomas, preached from its pulpit, adding steel no doubt to the hearts of his parishioners.

Today, come what might, the church of St Hywyn manages to maintain an unerring balance between the local community and the visitor, between worship and education, vitality and repose. Seeming hardly ever to rest, it preserves, none the less, a palpable air of tranquillity.

Richard Robert Jones

One of Aberdaron's best-known characters was a strange, dishevelled-looking individual who would wander round dressed in a rabbit-fur hat with upturned ears and an old military coat, the pockets of which were stuffed with well-thumbed books and numerous cats.

He carried with him a battered french horn and should you ever meet him, he would probably break into a recitation in a foreign tongue. He would read your palm and offer to tidy your garden.

So, who was this odd, unnerving fellow? Some thought him a rejected university lecturer or an officer from a faraway place, while others claimed he was a person of noble birth who had suffered a mental breakdown.

But he was none of these. His name was Richard Robert Jones and he came from 'Cae'r Eos', a short distance from Aberdaron. His father, a carpenter, enraged by his son's desire to study, beat him without mercy: the boy's bread, they say, was 'steeped in tears'.

'Cae'r Eos', Dic Aberdaron's home. rhiw.com

One day, Richard ran away from home, became a vagrant and began to tend gardens in return for books and food. Languages were his passion and he could soon speak 13 or 14 fluently. On one occasion, as he rested from his labours, someone asked him what he was reading. It was a book of Ethiopian grammar!

Richard Jones – known as Dic Aberdaron – spent many years wandering from town to town, and he was seen in places as far apart as Liverpool and London. He died in 1843 in St Asaph at the age of 63.

Promenade:

Aberdaron to Mynydd Mawr

While its existence is implicit, you cannot actually see Ynys Enlli – the 'kingdom' of Bardsey – from Aberdaron. For the best mainland view of the island (though nothing can compare with the uplifting sea crossing), you must go to Mynydd Mawr.

Through Bardsey Sound. Oliver Hodgson

Ynys Enlli, burial place of '20,000 saints'.
Oliver Hodgson

A cliff walk – beginning at the steps of Porth Simdde, the chimney – will lead you there. It can be quite demanding: high above the sea, dropping to the shore; the path now faint and evasive, now unambiguous and confident; allowing a view here, denying a glimpse there; hanging over Ynys Piod (Magpie Island) and falling steeply to Porth Meudwy, where – timelessly – fishermen still make ready their lobster pots and cobble their boats. The pilgrims, it is claimed, would have sailed across the Sound to Ynys Enlli from here – and today, at far less risk, you can do the same.

Now climb again, over Porth Cloch – the cemetery of Bala Abbey's great bell – above the knotty crags of Craig Cwlwm and the cliffs of Porth y Pistyll, past the seals of Carreg Ddu, up to Gallows Point and beyond the chicken pond, to the slopes of the great mountain itself...

You may, however, adopt a less exacting route.

Walk or drive along the steeply-climbing lane that winds westwards from Aberdaron. Fork left after half a mile – near the site of Ffynnon Saint – and head for Uwchmynydd. You will soon pass the turn off for Porth Meudwy (and, indeed, for Cwrt – the court house for the mediaeval manor of Enlli) and Penryhyn Bach on your left. Carry on over the cattle grid, and, picking your way among the sheep, cross the heath (resplendent in late summer with 'great banks of purple and gold') and behold! Two miles offshore, splendidly riding the seas, the great shadowy whale back of Ynys Enlli.

Now, on the high storm-stripped slopes of Mynydd Mawr – the anatomy of the land laid bare behind you, its spirit captured in the island before you – you are close to what would have been the end of the pilgrims' overland journey; close to the half-concealed remains of Capel Mair – St Mary's chapel – where they would have prayed for safe passage through the hostile currents of the Swnt; close to the yellow standing stone, Maen Melyn, which would have marked their arrival here; and close to Ffynnon Fair – St Mary's Well – where legends were created and spirits restored.

If the seas are moderate, scramble down to that miraculous well – its waters fresh or salty according to the tide – and anticipate, as the pilgrims may have done, the hazards that lie ahead. Relish the visceral, biting, pre-Cambrian rawness of this ancient place, and imagine the awe and wonder of those heroic travellers.

Maen Melyn, the pilgrims' stone, Mynydd Mawr.

Porth Ysgaden.
Catriona and Rodney Bracewell

XII Llanllawen to Porth Dinllaen

Return to Uwchmynydd to continue your journey. Before proceeding along the coast, however, allow yourself a short detour to Porth Llanllawen. It is remote and silent, a whole universe away from the clamour of Abersoch just a few miles beyond the ridge.

Sit down on the rocks for a few moments and absorb the atmosphere... listen... nothing!

Well, almost nothing. You may in fact hear the faintest swish of the waves, but that's all... except for the hum of an insect and the distant squawk of a chough or gull. Certainly nothing more... unless you count the hiss of shells drawn down the beach, the changing notes of the breeze and – barely perceptible – the barking of a seal.

Celebration at Llanllawen Fawr, by F.H. May.
rhiw.com

Llanllawen: truly a place for the senses! Look, listen, touch, smell, taste – the sand and shingle and soil; the stone, the salt, the squall; the thrift and gorse. Touch the honeycombed rocks of prehistory. Feel the dormant spirits of Stone, Iron and Bronze. Sniff the clean wind from Ireland.

To continue!

You will soon be heading along the coast to Porth Dinllaen. But first there is the small matter of Mynydd Anelog. True, there are perfectly convenient routes to both east and west, but the question is, as the mountain looms, can you resist the call of its summit? Let us assume you can't!

Mynydd Anelog, though not high, affords one of Llŷn's best-drawn views. See the lanes wandering past Carreg and Rhydlios; pulling aside from the sheer rocks; veering first one way then another. Notice how they follow the contours to Llithfaen, disappear between Rival peaks, and fall into the shadowy gorge between Tre'r Ceiri and Bwlch Mawr. See the road coming over from Aberdaron, passing through Tudweiliog to Edern, maintaining a distant rapport with the coast; struggling trees leaning from the wind; field walls – cloddiau – making mysterious patterns; sheep, sheltered in their lee. Before you descend, look towards Garn Fadryn and be reminded of the beginning of your journey.

Aber Geirch.
Catriona and Rodney Bracewell

April sunshine, whistling sands.
Oliver Hodgson

This is a moody, lonely coast, its paths often far removed from the civility of country lane and hedgerow. Roads hardly ever touch its coves, and where they do, they bring little traffic. Given the shore's countless chicanes and sidesteps, you may walk 15 or 20 miles without sight or sound of village; without refreshment. And, even in the height of the season, human company may be at a premium.

Embraced by generic virtues of remoteness and beauty, the ports and beaches from Llanllawen to Dinllaen are, nevertheless, highly distinctive. A handful offer reasonable access for the motorist – although approach lanes tend to be narrow and car parks rare.[19] Bus services, however – a practicable alternative – cover much of the area.

The coastal walk to Porth Dinllaen might seem a little daunting, but it is something you will never forget. Especially during those long winter evenings when you are many miles away.

Then, you will recall the red jasper cliffs at Carreg and the family who lived in the farm there for – what was it? – 600 years. You will remember coming round the headland to Porth Oer – magical solitude one moment, a beach sprinkled with holidaymakers the next! How you

'My father, the schoolmaster of Llangwnnadl', writes Gwilym Jones, 'at the wheel of his Horstman Cycle car.'

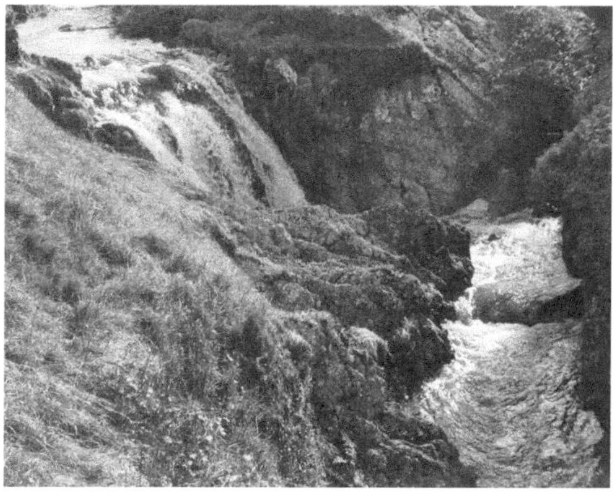

walked on the squeaky sands and defied anyone to describe them as 'whistling'. The Penllech waterfall gushing across the shore. Miranda's pony and trap. The old coal yards at Porth Ysgaden and the headland's weather-beaten wall. The detours you made to see John Gwyndaf's cottage garden and the lonely dingle church at Llangwnnadl. The magnetic rock, the pilgrims' signposts, and Yr Eifl – the Rivals – ever more dominant, marshalling themselves into new compositions with your every step.

Above left: The gardeners of Cefnamwlch dressed, as you see, for a spot of light gardening.

Gwilym Jones

Above: The Penllech waterfall.

The 'Garibaldi' under repair at Ysgaden.

Gwilym Jones

'Felin Penllech', home of author Gwilym Jones. His mother and grandmother can be seen standing in the doorway. An upper storey was added to the house in 1931.

Below: The Tudweiliog cobbler, Thomas Hughes, with friends.

Gwilym Jones

Below right: Chris 'Santa' Pitts, about to take to the water.

John Gwyndaf Roberts in his Tudweiliog garden. John has lived in the cottage for nearly 70 years.

Borth Wen and Porth Dinllaen.

Catriona and Rodney Bracewell

Saturday. The Tir Gwenith coach. Its passengers included the local preacher doing his weekend rounds.

An Entertaining and Instructive Visit to Tudweiliog

Tudweiliog's first motor bus. What an occasion.

courtesy Gwilym Jones

After several days we ventured inland from Porth Tywyn to Tudweiliog, a rare village bestriding the road from Aberdaron. It is a village coupled with the Wynne-Finch family from nearby Cefnamwlch, a family variously described as generous, altruistic and art-loving.

Although we were strangers – and fairly bedraggled ones at that – the villagers we encountered were the very model of kindliness, most, if not all of them, demonstrating nothing of the guarded insularity we might have expected of them. In the village hostelry, for example, we were astonished to find not only the landlord, but

Tudweiliog's old White Horse tavern, located where the Post Office now stands.

also his fellows turning from their native Welsh to English, the lighter to make of what they may have sensed as our unease.

One young man, charmingly loquacious, soon monopolised our company with tales of local characters and events: of two lads – John Jones and T.J. Roberts – who, while out fishing, lost their oars, drifted out to sea and ended up heroes on Irish shores; the wrecked whisky ship whose cargo somehow found its way into houses for miles around, effecting months of unmitigated merriment; the loss of the good ship *Cyprian*, whose captain selflessly assigned his life jacket to a young stowaway but paid for his charity with his own life.

That night we lodged in pleasant rooms, and the next morning, after a prodigious breakfast, the talkative young fellow accompanied us back to the shore, his commentary at least as assiduous as it had been the previous evening. Animated accounts escorted our every step: the rock at Porth Tywyn which had somehow become associated with forecasting local market prices; the Wynne-Finch family's genteel picnics on the headland at Porth Ysgaden, and so forth.

T.J. Roberts and John Jones after their frightening ordeal.

It was both entertaining and most instructive. And when we finally took our leave of the spirited young gent, we did so with the utter conviction that not a single inch of this quiet corner of Llŷn is without incident!

High tide at Tŷ Coch.

XIII Porth Dinllaen

Once you have negotiated the morass of Borth Wen, the fresh, gusty approaches to Porth Dinllaen are a delight: hard, spiky rocks, spotless shingle, scrubbed grass, laundered sand.

Turn north towards Carreg Ddu, circumnavigate the golf course. Out on the horizon, Caergybi – the holy head of Môn. Look north-east towards the Rivals – grand, and seeming arrogant in their judicial wigs of cloud; step down to the lifeboat house, past the long finger jetty. Single file.

Coming now to Hen Borth: the old cottages clustered in a semi-circle of shrubs, tight against their guardian cliffs, looking across the sandy crescent to Pen Cim, Bwlch, Penrhyn Nefyn and the rising sun. Below, in tall white letters, Tŷ COCH writ large on the

August Bank Holiday.

'Whitehall'. Peter Leslie

roof of the inn; along the shore, trailers, fish crates, tractors, boats upturned like cockleshells; a handsome stone house – called 'Whitehall' with brazen incongruity! The high tides lap its burly terrace, and sometimes creep through the arch and into the courtyard.

Like the castle at Cricieth, like Ynys Enlli and Yr Eifl, Porth Dinllaen[20] is one of Penrhyn Llŷn's definitive images. Seeming blissfully idyllic, she gazes contentedly upon the world from a thousand postcards, calendars, glossy brochures and chocolate boxes. Porth Dinllaen is, in short, the adman's dream, the poet's muse, the apple of the artist's eye. Yet although over the years numerous commentators have applauded her beauty, others have adopted different perspectives. Many make reference to 'the port that never was', while in one instance, a certain 'Eminent Welsh Historian'[21] describes Porth Dinllaen as 'a place which nature intended to have a history but which never did.'

Fortunately, the books of local author Tom Morris have demonstrated the folly of this assessment.[22] Scholarly, comprehensive and containing the intimate perceptions of someone born and brought

Below: the 'Whitehall' arch. Gwilym Jones

Below right: A Southampton flying boat descends upon Porth Dinllaen. Gwilym Jones

up in the area, Mr Morris's accounts focus not so much upon the picture-postcard village as on the community; the living, working organism; its past and its present.

Ships, inevitably, loom large. They were built on the beach here – 50 and more – wherever a firm and even surface could be found. No aristocratic beauties, these were tubby, flat-bottomed commoners – usually schooners or sloops – built to take the knocks of shallow landings, to labour long and hard, and to knuckle under. And while their builders – men like Evan Ellis, Hugh Hughes, James Owen – measured and agonised, David Rice Hughes of Bwlch would shape and sew their sails, and poets would compose verses to be recited as the new vessels were dragged on rollers across the sand to the sea.

At the same time, a fair variety of cargoes trundled in and out of Porth Dinllaen; corn, salt, barley, bricks for Swansea, coal from Liverpool, culm from Llanelli or Neath, limestone from Cork. Loading, unloading, taking ballast, laying to; fishing boats lying in wait or landing catches; farmers queuing to fill their carts with soap shavings for the fields. A buzz of lime kilns and curing sheds; a brick factory and a customs house.

Beside which, all the fuss and bother of an ebullient community. Galas, brawls, weddings, burials. Characters and events springing from the ledgers of history, a match for anyone anywhere. Seafarers, wives and fishwives, reprobates, heroes. Jane Ellen Jones, landlady of Tŷ Coch and harbourmaster; Griffith Hughes, Methodist minister and entrepreneur; Cliff Webley, landlord and raconteur. The seaplanes disaster, the beaching of the *Matje*; lifeboats *Barbara Fleming* and *Hetty Rampton*, and their fearless crews; filmstar Demi Moore standing with Brione Webley at the bar of

Three studies of Porth Dinllaen.

rhiw.com

A church outing.

rhiw.com

Tŷ Coch; the 10 fishermen and six boats that still work from these shores and the tourists who flock to Porth Dinllaen in their thousands.

That is history, Mr 'Eminent Historian'. How could you have missed it?

Yet, Porth Dinllaen's historical resonance might so easily have been different. Early in the 19th century as a contestant in the race to establish a major port for the Irish sea crossing, Dinllaen's selection for this role was regarded by many as almost a foregone conclusion. For which of her rivals – Holyhead, Caernarfon and Liverpool among them – could offer comparable facilities and potential? Holyhead seemed particularly deficient. Sited upon a small, remote islet off the north-west coast of Anglesey (itself separated from the mainland by the turbulent, unbridged Menai Strait), Holyhead's credentials were derisory. As for other candidates, they hardly warranted serious discussion since they, too, appeared, in their several ways, ripe for elimination.

Porth Dinllaen on the other hand, a safe and shallow harbour not more than 100 paces from deep water, could proffer every advantage. Statistics regarding traffic movement in 1804 were quite staggering. It was by no means unusual to find up to 100 ships crowding the shallows while 100 more awaited entry. There was an efficient pier, a good system for loading and unloading (for both passengers and cargo) and ample accommodation for travellers. Furthermore, approach roads, both extant and proposed, guaranteed modern, convenient access.

Further afield, Mr Madocks's bold crossing of Traeth Mawr had virtually revolutionised communications both within and far beyond Wales. London was now easily reached; a railway line could not be far behind. Nor had official support been reticent. Turnpike Trust, Harbour Board and various other agencies had endorsed Porth Dinllaen's claim, and even a formal enquiry had delivered a positive judgement.

One could only marvel at the foresight and energy of Mr Madocks. He had prepared the ground with such diligence, acquiring land for development, unceasingly negotiating with relevant organisations and individuals, creating in Tre Madoc a comfortable staging post, and even saluting Dublin and London in the streets of his borough. What more could the fellow have done! Taking all of this into account, it was generally assumed that within two or three years, Porth Dinllaen would be among the busiest and richest ports in the land.

Yet the quirks of history cannot be predicted, and Porth Dinllaen's fortunes were to be unceremoniously crushed when, in 1819, Thomas Teford – having been appointed to survey communications within North Wales – built a suspension bridge across the Menai Strait. Completed in 1826, the bridge revived Holyhead's ambitions, and, in due course, she and not Port Dinllaen won selection – by a single parliamentary vote – as the primary port for Ireland.

In 1850 Robert Stephenson's Britannia railway bridge completed the communications jigsaw, and Porth Dinllaen, having no part to play, retired into picturesque isolation.

Promenade: Porth Dinllaen to Nefyn

Leave Porth Dinllaen either by the lane behind Tŷ Coch – which will lead you past the golf club pavilion and on to Morfa Nefyn – or by walking along the beach to the big white house at Bwlch (possibly a more appealing alternative).

On the left, gently sloping sands; to the right, high, porous, 'unstable' cliffs, pock-marked with nesting burrows; and, all around, grey, blue and speckled pebbles, shelves of whittled sand and bright orange crab shells stripped of nourishment. Follow the path past the rock pools over Pen Cim and see the *SS Dora Warehouse* – perched, to this day, on its pillars and reflected in the shallows. Imagine the old steamers hooting and drawing up alongside the jetty to deliver the groceries. Carry on past 'Hen Blass' – the good-times tavern – and head for 'Tŷ Newydd', the big white house at Bwlch, behind which – in the 'Gegin' – once stood Roland Williams's Sunday School.

Tanrallt Tavern, now 'Hen Blas'.

Gwilym Jones

Leave the shore here and climb the 73 tidy steps to the cliff top. (Thirteen more steps, incidentally, will take you to the Cliffs Inn.) The coastal path – well travelled – now wanders towards Nefyn, passing, on its way, a number of strategically-placed benches, memorials to people who 'loved this place'. And not only people! One dedication reads:

To Higgins Greenhalgh –
we didn't have the heart
to tell him he was a dog.

Take stock, take a seat, look round: Penrhyn Nefyn, Gwylwyr Carreglefain, an outstretched ocean...

Climb down to the harbour, browse among the boats. Cross the bay towards the town high on the cliff, make your way up the crooked lane (Lôn Gam)...and soon you will come to the province of Herring.

Boats and Rivals.

rhiw.com

Porth Nefyn.

Gwilym Jones

St David's Church.

St Mary's Church, down in the old town…Its ship-in-full-sail weathervane spinning and squeaking aimlessly in the wind.

Cath Hope

XIV Nefyn

'The only settlements of any size on the north coast, declares *The Rough Guide to Wales*[23], 'are a pair of villages (Nefyn and Morfa Nefyn) overlooking beautiful sweeping bays. Nefyn is the larger, but it does not have a lot to recommend it. You can, however, learn about the village's herring-fishing past in the mildly diverting Maritime Museum.'

It is easy to underestimate Nefyn. An independent, take-it-or-leave-it kind of a place, the town's visual features, though by no means unpleasant, hardly quicken the pulse: a watchtower scanning the horizon, tidy modern houses and fine old ones, the Nanhoron Hotel, a handsome new church – St David's – detached from its churchyard, an ancient well and a busy crossing of cramped, traffic-squeezed streets. Y Groes – the cross – and, down in the old town, St Mary's Church and Maritime Museum barred and fenced off, its ship-in-full-sail weathervane spinning and squeaking aimlessly in the wind.

However, Nefyn is deceptive, for it is a town cradling a distinction far greater than the sum of its parts; a treasure trove awaiting discovery, abounding in names and symbols of an eventful, often glorious past:

Bryn Mynach, Monks' Hill – shadows of a mediaeval priory…

The spirit of St Nefyn buried somewhere in the very fabric of St Mary's Church…

Pilgrims gathered at the well…

A motte and bailey castle, where now the watchtower stands…

Nefyn, power base for Gryffydd ap Cynan – future prince of Gwynedd…

Giraldus Cambrensis (Gerald of Wales) and Archbishop Baldwin of Canterbury, recruiting soldiers for the Third Crusade. Resting here on Palm Sunday, 1188. How many good men of Nefyn face Saladin the Infidel and live to tell the tale…

'Cae Iorwerth' and 'Cae Ymryson' – Edward's Field and the Field of the Contest – King Edward I choosing to celebrate what he believes to be the conquest of the Welsh! There is a great tournament here, and a glittering royal encampment is spread across this windswept plateau…

1355: the Black Prince made Nefyn (together with Pwllheli, its smaller neighbour) a Royal Borough, one of only 10 in the whole of Wales. The town's revenue is assigned to a certain Nigel de Lohareyn, who collects his dues and does as he pleases…

Would you trust this man? An English view of the 'typical Welshman' – one shoe on, one shoe off, bad hair!

Glyndŵr's men – sensing perhaps a growing Englishness – setting fire to the town and almost destroying it…

Nefyn lies dormant until the 16th century. And then, it stirs. It prospers. Shipbuilding, seamanship and trading intensify. The people of the town are quick-witted and sound of judgment. Yet, above all else, it is one commodity that makes Nefyn fat: herring. For many a century herrings are the lords of the table, darlings of the exchequer. Five thousand barrels are exported in 1747. Herrings with 'backs like farmers' and 'bellies like publicans' adorn the town's crest, and are held

Penwaig Nefyn – The herrings of Nefyn.

rhiw.com

Three plump, cheerful herrings smiling down upon Stryd y Ffynnon… yesterday's men.

Timeless Nefyn!

in such esteem that the townsfolk themselves become known as Penwaig Nefyn – Herrings of Nefyn.

Notwithstanding obvious dissimilarities, Nefyn and Pwllheli would seem to have much in common. Neither town is ostentatious, neither inclined to exaggerate its merits. Both, resolute in the face of today's challenges, have remained champions of Welsh language and culture.

Yet, inevitably, their fortunes have diverged, and while Pwllheli marches on, a vibrant market place, Nefyn, more isolated, has taken a different path. The shipyards and trading posts have long departed, the museum is locked, the salt cottages abandoned, and though lobsters, whelks and velvet crabs do what they can to uphold Nefyn's time-honoured fishing tradition, their task is steep.

True, three plump, cheerful herrings continue to smile down upon Stryd y Ffynnon, but, to be honest, theirs is a fools' paradise. Surely they know they are yesterday's men.

If one could only spirit away the omnipresent motor vehicle, Stryd y Ffynnon – Well Street – would look much as it did 100 years ago: on the left, the well itself, 'Three Herrings' to the right and ahead, two lines of buildings, varying in height and projection, leading, via the chapel and the Nanhoron Clock, to the turning for Pistyll, Llithfaen and all points north and east.

You may, however, have decided at Traeth Nefyn to bypass the town altogether, and to continue eastwards along the beach (a rugged beach it is too!) If so, you will probably have to leave the shore where the stream runs down from Wern, since, in front of you, Penrhyn Bodeilas may offer stern resistance.

Go through the holiday park at Wern and intercept the pilgrims' path from Nefyn, which, skirting the western flank of Gwylwyr Carreglefain, crosses the road and drops below the village of Pistyll. You will pass the remnants of a hut circle (once used as a cock-fighting pit), a ghostly, abandoned hotel and a mill pool. You will now see, tucked away in a fold of hills, St Beuno's Church.

Stryd y Ffynnon, Well Street, Nefyn, early in the 20th century.

Leaving Nefyn, heading for Wern.

The abandoned hotel at Pistyll.

St Beuno's Church.

Peter Leslie

PILGRIMS' RETREAT

Founded in the Middle Ages, this was a hospice church for weary pilgrims; a retreat or resting place for the old and infirm; a refuge for lepers. There was a priory and an inn here, a well for pure, fresh water and, on a nearby hill, shelters for the sick. Medicinal plants grew in abundance, and the remains of a herb plantation may still be seen.

If you come here at Christmas or at Easter, or if you visit at Lammas – the feast of the first fruits of August – you may find the church's west door framed with boughs of holly or eucalyptus. Inside, the floor will be strewn with rushes and sweet-smelling herbs. Flowers of the village will decorate the lepers' window and the ancient Celtic font, while a garland of fern will encircle the faded mural. Shafts of light from narrow windows will accentuate the shadows of the roof timbers and the unevenness of the rough-hewn walls.

The interior of St Beuno's Church.

Peter Leslie

It is said that St Beuno himself (whom we shall meet again at Clynnog Fawr) was laid to rest beneath this very altar.[24]

Promenade:
St Beuno's to Nant Gwrtheyrn

Carreg y Llam from Porth y Nant.

rhiw.com

The footpath from the church will wind over the hill to an intersection at Ciliau Canol. Turn left here to visit the sea bird colony at Carreg y Llam and to enjoy – if enjoy is the word – the dizzying heights of the formidable cliffs. It is a dramatic scene, a drama magnified, if luck obliges, by the sight of Irish mountains crouching black on the horizon.

Moel Ty-gwyn behind you; Gwynus too. And ahead, stark, battle-hardened mountains, shorn of vegetation, claiming the foreground, imposing themselves, presiding over climate and light, and, not least, playing extraordinary tricks with perceptions of scale. See the westernmost Rival swooping down into the waves. Can it truly be only 1,500ft from summit to sea?

To return to the shore from Carreg y Llam, go back to the intersection and head for Ciliau Isaf. Turn left and pick up the track to Porth y Nant.

Carreg y Llam.

Oliver Hodgson

Cottages of Sea View and Mountain View.

Peter Leslie

XV Nant Gwrtheyrn (Vortigern's Valley)

Over the heath and beyond the woodland at Gallt y Bwlch, the land – gritty and worn – is littered with reminders of the people who would once have worked here: hoists and winding wheels, vertical, half-split faces of rock, hasps of rusting iron, hulks of granite, company workshops grafted to the mountain – rock on rock, tumbledown sheds and gaping doorways; in the distance, deserted farmsteads and age-old field walls.

The old blacksmith shop, Nant quarry.

rhiw.com

And finally – when and where you might least have expected it – a village appearing over the rim of the plateau. It stands some way above the sea at the foot of Nant Gwrtheyrn – Vortigern's Valley – and is three parts surrounded by what would appear to be insuperable mountains. This is the former quarry village of Porth y Nant: an isolated community seemingly quite independent of the outside world.

Tŷ Hen. rhiw.com

Little by little, as you ascend the path from Quarry Beach, the village takes shape: 'Tŷ Hen' – the old house – derelict, picturesque; Caffi Meinir, on the site of 'Tŷ Hen's' former outbuildings; Cae Mawr, the big, open field, and – within the boundary wall – Cae Bach; looking across Cae Bach, at right angles to one another, two rows of terraced cottages – Mountain View and Sea View – the village square at their confluence; the office – at Bay View; to the west, beyond the compound – discrete and dignified – the Plas, or Mansion, every inch an aristocrat; and finally, in the far corner, raised above the level of the houses, the chapel – now a Heritage Centre – light, airy and perfectly groomed.

Of course, time was when Evan Wynne's shop, George Matts's little red hut, not to mention a village store and bake house, would sustain 200 people here; when sledges would rattle down the rough track from Llithfaen, top-heavy with sideboards and kitchen tables; when steamers would tie in at the jetty with coal and timber; when not one, but three granite quarries – Porth y Nant, Carreg y Llam and Cae'r Nant – would create prosperity for all, and the noises of works' hooters, rock blasting, workers' chitchat and children's laughter would merge and bounce off mountain walls; when the Plas would sing with the music of Company receptions; when 'Nant' – as the village was affectionately known – was a resonant, multi-lingual community 'with Welsh, Irish and English families living side by side in harmony'.[25]

Nant. Cath Hope

Ken Earp and Bobi Hughes deliver the groceries.

Gwyn Ellis

Mr Jones, the minister, and the pupils of 1898.

Gwyn Ellis

Mary Roberts with her class of 1938.

Gwyn Ellis

It has been noted, however (with almost equal measures of vexation and approval), that an inn was not provided. Now, for those who would enjoy an occasional glass of ale, this was a matter of some concern, for the nearest inn, the 'Vic', was over the mountain in Llithfaen.

Imagine it: the punishing climb from the village, the slippery, winding track, sheer – one in three in some places – uneven and acutely unsympathetic to travellers of any kind. And think of the journey home – a little 'over-the-eight' perhaps, unsteady, giddy. How the ground would fall away, how the shadows would spring sickeningly to life. How Mrs Butler's icy ghost, not to say Mr Barlow's haunted tree, would lie in wait for the fuddled, bleary-eyed reveller. Never has the phrase 'rolling home' seemed more appropriate.

While inspiring an abundance of colourful and affectionate memories, everyday life in the valley must have been anything but idyllic: hardly the place, one would have thought, for the weak, the idle, the self-centred. For all its sunshine, companionship and merriment, this was, after all, a 'dark, deep and horrid' place, a 'blasted heath' of 'black precipices', remorseless rains and pitiless cold, where, in the blink of any eye, the Barracks (the village's first row of cottages) could be swept to destruction in a sea of mud, or the wooden school be seized by the neck and tossed up into the sky on a northern gale.

And there were other things. The body on the beach. The jetty disaster. Quarry dissolution. The haunted house at Cae'r Nant. It must sometimes almost have seemed that the whole valley was cursed…

Mrs Williams – Llithfaen-bound.

Gwilym Jones

And indeed it was.

But before we speak of curses, we have a king to acknowledge.

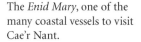

The *Enid Mary*, one of the many coastal vessels to visit Cae'r Nant.

Gwilym Jones

Field patterns of Nant.

VORTIGERN

This rok is called Guotheren –
ie Vallis Vortigerni in Llene...

So wrote Renaissance traveller John Leland on his visit to Llŷn in the 1530s. But who is the 'Vortigerni' and how can his name have become enshrined in this place?

We look back to AD450: a restless England, torn with dissention. The Celtic King Vortigern of Wessex, 'a warrior tall and strong', has formed a Council of Elders in a bid to neutralise threats from the Picts and Irish. But now jealous intrigues abound, the King's authority is undermined and in desperation he turns to the Saxons for support. A banquet is arranged to celebrate this unlikely alliance, the seating plan – Saxon, Briton, Saxon, Briton – a touching symbol of brotherhood. The occasion proceeds splendidly until, at a given signal, each Saxon draws a dagger and slays his neighbour. It is an event known to history as 'the treachery of the long knives'.

The King himself is spared, and when he lamely surrenders his kingdom in return for survival, his people declare him traitor. He has sacrificed language, culture and race.

The King, a broken man, is cast out. He roams far and wide, accompanied by his daughter Madryn and a few faithful friends.

Eventually, they reach a deep silent valley at the farthest edge of Wales. Their journey is done. Madryn settles at a hill fort, now called Garn Fadryn, while her father builds a wooden castle in the valley, the 'rok called Guotheren,' Vortigern's Valley.

As for the King's demise, some say his enemies sought him out and slew him as he looked out to sea, others that his feeble castle was struck and 'consumed by lightning'.

You may be sceptical dear reader, but note this. Several centuries later, a stone coffin containing the bones of a tall man was discovered in a part of the valley now called Bedd Gwrtheyrn.[26] Upon the coffin lid was a Celtic inscription meaning VORTIGERN.

The Curses

To return now, however, to the curses of Nant Gwrtheyrn.

Long after the death of King Vortigern, a community of simple fisher folk settle in the valley. Seeing that they are pagans, three monks from St Beuno's cell at Clynnog Fawr take it upon themselves to convert them to Christianity. The holy men are, however, received with hostile indignation. Stones are thrown, and, in fear for their lives, they flee to the high ground. Here, emboldened by safe distance, they take courage, and resolve to curse these shameless and ungrateful heathens.

From afar, they address the fisher folk in masterful voice. 'No one born in this godless place shall ever lie in consecrated ground', thunders the first monk. 'Never shall man and woman born here of the same family be joined together in marriage', cries the second monk. 'This vile ungodly valley shall live thrice and shall die thrice and will at last become an abandoned ruin', roars the third monk.

Their day's work thus complete, the three pious men are satisfied, and they return to Clynnog secure in the knowledge that even though they have been unable to save the poor heathens' souls, they have at least found the wit and courage to consign them and their successors to damnation.

In the fullness of time the curses begin to discharge their duties. Fishermen, drowned at sea, are denied holy burial; womenfolk and children, bereft and hopeless, desert the valley. The village perishes.

In due course, however, a farming community makes its home in Vortigern's field. Among its number are cousins Rhys and Meinir, a young couple who fall in love and – unaware of the monks' curse – plan to marry.

Tradition dictates that on the day of the wedding, the groom must wait at the altar while the bride hides away. Friends will seek her out and carry her, joyfully, to the church. But Meinir conceals herself to such effect that she cannot be found. Darkness comes, the next day passes, and still there is neither sight nor sign of Rhys's bride. Days turn into weeks, and the young man, inconsolable, edges towards madness.

In turmoil, he leaves his home and, day and night, stands vigil beside the oak tree where he and Meinir had first declared their love. One afternoon, a tremendous storm breaks from the sky. As the thunder rolls, a sudden fork of lightning tears open the lovers' tree. There, inside, is the ensnared skeleton of Meinir. It is too much for Rhys to bear. He cries out and falls dead.

Haunted by these terrible things, the villagers begin to move away. For the second time, the valley is abandoned.

Two centuries later the quarry village of Porth y Nant is built. Its fortunes ebb and flow until, finally, in 1959, it too dwindles and dies, its 'cottage windows gazing like black, sightless eyes into the north wind'.

Pass the chapel and the old farmsteads, and walk up the hill towards Llithfaen, the zigzag lane almost Alpine in gradient and spectacle, the old sledge-trail (steeper still) crossing over from time to time; quarry headlands encircled by sea birds and thrashed by white breakers emerging as you ascend. Trees – tall and slender, alien and indigenous – furnish the great, flowing sweeps of hillside, and sheep-dotted heathland rises towards rock walls and galleries.

The village of Nant Gwrtheyrn became, in 1982, the Welsh Language and Heritage Centre.
Oliver Hodgson

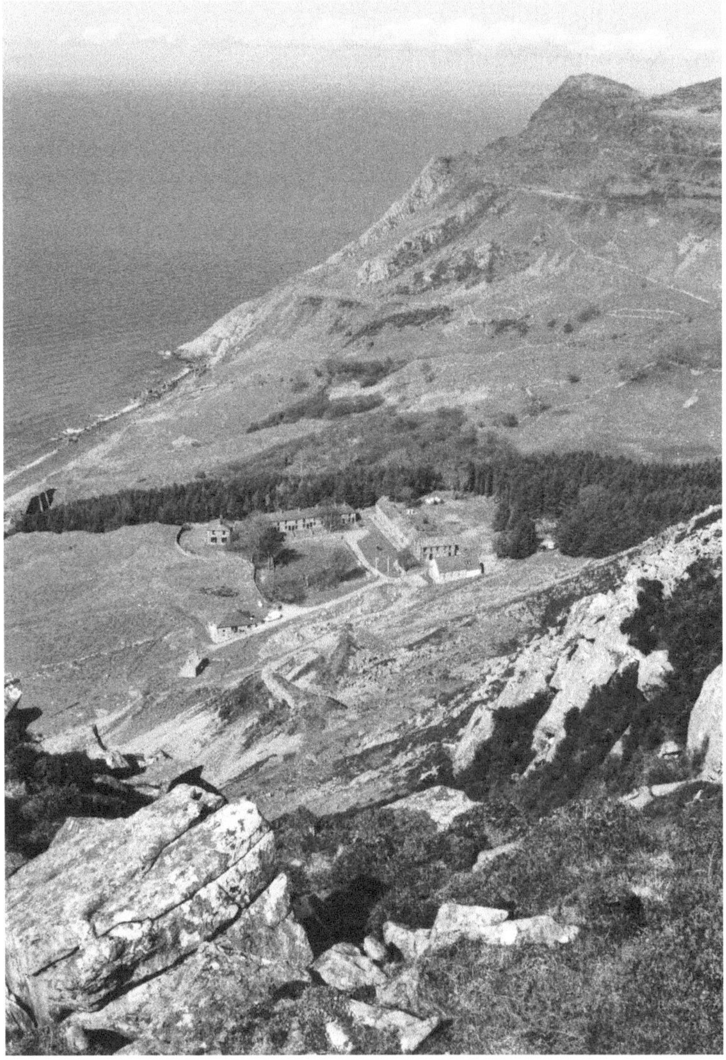

Stop at the second bend high above the village, its curses now disarmed. Look out over the valley, and what you see is a microcosm of Penrhyn Llŷn: myth, legend, romance; sea and mountain; relics of everyday life. All set in a landscape of stunning natural beauty. How fitting it is that in 1982, the village should be reborn under the happiest of circumstances as a centre for the study of the Welsh language and for the preservation of Wales's heritage;[27] yet how ironic that the name it bears is that of the ancient king who abandoned his homeland and yielded his own heritage to his enemy!

The *Amy Summerfield.*

THE *AMY SUMMERFIELD* STORY

as told by Gwilym Jones

On 22 March 1951 the 407-ton steam-driven coastal trader, the *Amy Summerfield*, left the River Mersey bound for the shore of the Llyn Peninsula, for her weekly visit to Cae'r Nant Quarry for a load of granite. It was a blustery morning with high gusts of wind.

On arriving at her destination, weather conditions were so atrocious that – for fear of his vessel colliding – the captain decided against approaching the loading jetty.

A few hours later the *Amy Summerfield* was safely berthed back at Liverpool, the captain having to report his return empty-handed to the shop's owners, W.A. Savage and Co. He was severely reprimanded and threatened with instant dismissal if he did not return to the quarry and load up.

The following morning he was once again in the vicinity of the landing jetty, the weather conditions just as bad as – if not worse than – the previous day, with high winds driving the surf, creating clouds of spray, making visibility poor and the approach hazardous. A rope was thrown to the vessel by the loading gang on the jetty, but it fell short of its destination and dropped in the water, entangling itself in the propeller with a disastrous result. It snatched one of the propeller's three blades, shearing it off.

All power now lost, the *Amy Summerfield* – at the mercy of the elements – was thrown broad-side on to an outcrop of rocks before ploughing stern first into the jetty, threatening to demolish the wooden structure. Within a few days the insurance assessors visited the scene and declared the vessel a total wreck.

In due course, a scrap metal merchant from Harlech bought the ship with the idea of refloating the damaged hull and sailing it to Portdinorwic, where it could be broken up. Soon it was realised, however, that the little coaster was unrepairable and would never float again. She would have to be dismantled on site, an enormous undertaking as the equipment needed to carry out the work would have to be transported down the somewhat inaccessible track through the village of Nant Gwrtheyrn, while the salvaged sections would have to be carted back up. However, the scrap merchant – a Mr Williams – was a man of positive thinking. He bought a war surplus tracked vehicle, succeeded in getting it down to the beach and transported the remains of the *Amy* to awaiting lorries in Llithfaen.

In the meantime, Crofts, the owners of the quarry, were concerned that the stricken vessel could well do further damage to the jetty; it was also impossible to load other vessels, and an order was given that the *Amy* had to be moved away to a safe distance. As there was an ample supply of coal in the ship's bunkers, a good head of steam was raised, a chain and anchor were thrown out on the beach and, using the vessel's steam windlass, the *Amy* was dragged clear enough to satisfy the quarry owners.

Today, 55 years on, there are still remnants of the *Amy Summerfield* on the beach at Porth y Nant, a reminder of the foolishness of greed.

Promenade:
Nant Gwrtheyrn to Trefor

At the top of the hill you will emerge from the pitch-black forest into the white, open daylight, wondering perhaps, where next?

The options are both generous and diverse, and you may be excused uncertainty. Will you indulge your historical side with an expedition to Tre'r Ceiri, the Town of Giants? Your social side with a trip to the inn at Llithfaen? Or your travelling side by just pressing on?

To be honest, should you profess even a glimmer of historical curiosity, it would be almost criminal to ignore the Town of Giants standing so close and so imperiously at your side. The climb is moderate – the only difficulty a loose scree near the summit – yet it will bring you not only to a vantage point that transcends all others, but to an abandoned 'city' of pre-historic beginnings: 150 stone shelters, an encircling wall, a crowing cairn. A place of work and leisure inhabited for 1,000 years.

Left and below: Granite mountain.

Oliver Hodgson

Should you prefer, however, to dispense with prehistoric matters and, instead, to continue your journey, you may now return to the coastal path which leads away from Nant Gwrtheyrn car park via the solemn flanks of Graig Ddu and Bwlch, and descends, ultimately, to Trefor.

Trefor.

Catriona and Rodney Bracewell

XVI Trefor

But for now, the village lies far below – a granite-hued island in a leaf-green ocean. See it from the quarry's gallery beyond the summit mast. Stand on the very brink of the mountain, the gallery itself – a gloomy battleground of fallen rock, long shadows and unfinished business – lying spine-chillingly behind you.

You can see from up here that Trefor's first reference is not to the wider world, but to the mountain; that its lanes lead primarily not to other towns, but to the dock and the quarry; that the mountain and the village are irrevocably linked – the mountain as the village's creator, the village, ungratefully, the mountain's assailant. How fitting that such a place should take its very name from the quarry company's first manager, Trefor Jones.

The track to the quarry.

Oliver Hodgson

Looking back to the 19th century, can you not imagine Samuel Holland's satisfaction when he realises that the granite he has located here (in 1854) is of such quality that it can surface a busy city street for 20 years – four times longer than stone mined elsewhere? No wonder David Williams calls it the 'rock of ages'; no wonder Holland can hardly wait to open his Eifl account. Soon a legion of workers clambers over the heights, drilling and blasting, while below, a village – tight rows of inseparable cottages, chapels, a school – is built to accommodate them.

As early as 1863, an already spirited social life is augmented by James Cooke and John Sharpe, who form a village band – a band, as they are inclined to say, forged 'for quarrymen by quarrymen' – sensibly employing not dainty violins and whimsical oboes, but tough, no-frills brass instruments... fit for 'a working man's orchestra', as Geraint Jones

Quarry cottages, Trefor.

Oliver Hodgson

likes to call it. Seasoned and resilient. Hear them even now in the chapel of Bethlehem!

To reach Trefor you will have dropped down on the steep road from the mountain – the old trolley incline and the woods of Sychnant to your left. You will have passed the quarry yard – still turning out chippings and in-fill (not to mention the celebrated curling stones that gained Winter Olympic gold in 2002) – and will have come to the crossroads at the village centre. And perhaps you will see how it is that Canon Thomas of St George's was moved to comment that what makes Trefor so distinctive is that few people ever pass through it. Isolation makes of it a beginning and an end, and you may also feel that such a status has done the village no harm at all. It is friendly and confidential, a community defined, as it were, by its autonomy.

Quarryman's workplace.

Peter Leslie

Promenade:
Trefor to Clynnog Fawr

As regards your coastal progress, the leaving of Trefor could create some difficulty. Should you go down to the harbour at Allt y Môr, you will perhaps see how ungratifying it might be to follow the stony, mud-streaked shore on its long, relatively featureless journey to Aberdesach, and you may well now think how prudent it is that both the pilgrims' trail and the coastal path elect to bypass Trefor altogether – the first choosing instead to head across the hills to Llanaelhaearn, thence to Clynnog Fawr, the second, seeking greater glories by retreating into the mountains (Pen-llechog, Gyrn Ddu, Gyrn Goch, Bwlch Mawr), which now step back commandingly from the shore, before it too descends to

The jetty at Allt y Môr.

Above and below: The harbour at Trefor.

Peter Leslie

Clynnog. For the moment – though a new bypass will soon alleviate the risk – the alternative of following the main Caernarfon road should be explored cautiously, since this busy, narrow section is hardly suitable for the walker. Nevertheless, a thoughtful combination of footpath, lane and road is a distinct possibility.

Whatever your choice, you will by now have forsaken the ancient hundred of Llŷn, and you will have entered Arfon for what is the final part of your journey.

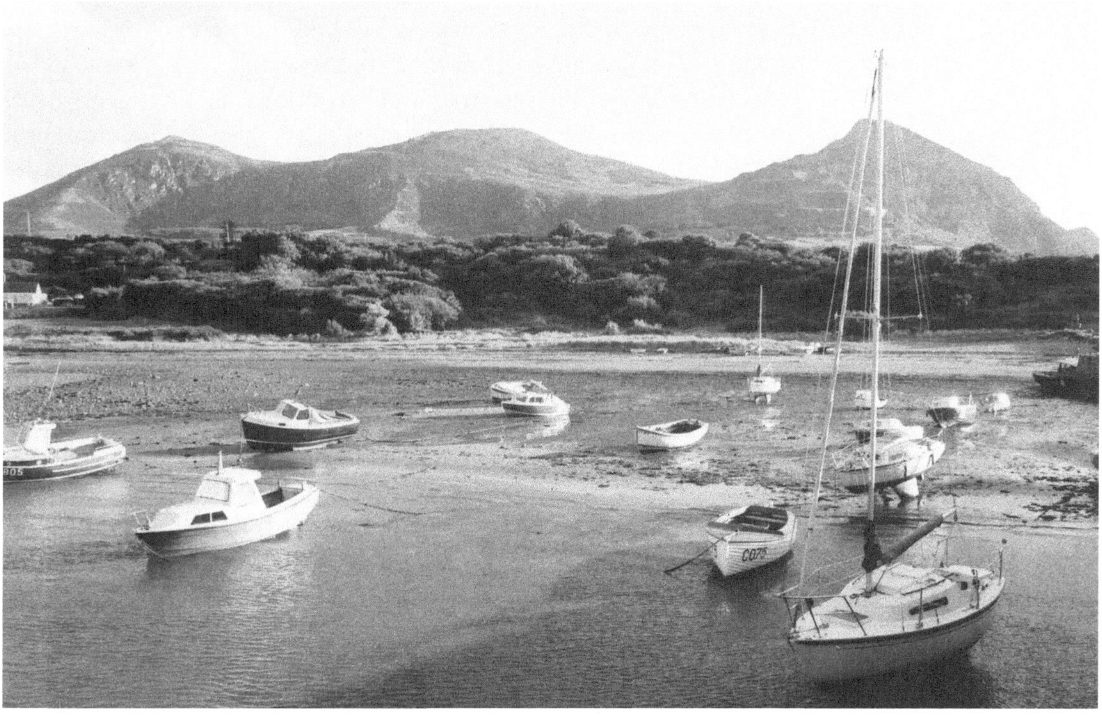

Clynnog Fawr.
Catriona and Rodney Bracewell

CLYNNOG FAWR

While the ecclesiastical architects of the Gothic Age tended to shun the saints of Penrhyn Llŷn, they appear to have made a notable exception for St Beuno.

Totally free of affectation and modestly positioned below the level of the road, St Beuno's Church at Clynnog Fawr – try though it might – cannot hope to disguise its magnificence. Step down into its churchyard and you cannot fail to be impressed by the broad perpendicular arch of its east window, the pinnacles and battlements, the buttressed tower. Cottages gather round it in the manner of a cathedral close, creating an impression of singular importance.

Y Beuno, an inn fit for a saint.

The village, Clynnog.

Sharron Jones

And so it should be for North Wales' greatest Celtic saint, a holy man of St David's calibre, and a teacher and healer so gifted that even the replacement of a severed head represented but a minor challenge.

The present church of St Beuno, built in the 16th century, stands on the site of the saint's seventh-century 'clas', or teaching monastery. Pilgrims would assemble here in preparation for their journey to Ynys Enlli, and it is no doubt their donations which allowed such a fine church to be raised. St Beuno's chest – carved from a single piece of oak – can be seen inside the building. It was in this 'treasury' that the monies were kept.

Above and below: The church of St Beuno, quite unable to disguise its magnificence.

Oliver Hodgson

The interior – both of the church itself and of the adjacent chapel – combines the grand and the simple, the monastic and the ornamental, with easy conviction: artefact and architecture as a single inspiration, lime, whitewash and naked stone, carved roof timbers, rood screen elaborations, the cross of the great pilgrimage, the saint's stone and – though one must call Pistyll to mind – the tomb of St Beuno himself! In the churchyard, a 10th-century sundial and along the road, as old as the hills, the saint's holy well.

Between Clynnog and Aberdesach, several shore-bound paths compete for your approval. But study them carefully, for, in the manner of many a path of Penrhyn Llŷn, some are by no means averse to the flattery of deception. The lane that sets out from beside the church, however, is both innocent in that respect and particularly pleasant. It even offers an added attraction, a well-preserved cromlech, or burial chamber, standing – half spectator, half custodian – above the waves. Farther on, near 'Ty'n-y-coed', a path leads down to Y Borth, a former site – though the sea has left us nothing – of a small group of fisherman's cottages. The shore here, though a little awkward to negotiate, is by no means impassable.

Cottages gather round the church in the manner of a cathedral close.

Oliver Hodgson

Heading north along the coast to Pontllyfni the walking is good.

From the seafront car park at Aberdesach, an iron footbridge leads off over the river, past a line of assorted holiday chalets and down to the shore. Look back via Bwlch Mawr and Gyrn Goch to Yr Eifl – rivals at peace, lazing in the sea. Ahead, in the shallow water, Trwyn Maen Dylan

The burial chamber at Clynnog Fawr.

– sometimes called lovers' rock – and a small stream spilling down from Bryncroes way. The sky is wide. Little wonder the Goddess of Light once played here. A curving stony shore with a hinterland of crumbling, receding cliffs will bring you to Pontllyfni beach.

Aberdesach, a gathering storm.
Oliver Hodgson

XVII Pontllyfni Beach

Variations on a theme.
Oliver Hodgson

Though it may seem improbable, the view from here is quite unlike any other we have encountered on our journey. Once again, Penrhyn Llŷn manages somehow to offer a new variation upon her perpetual theme of sea, shore and sky. Look north towards the motte at Dinas Dinlle: the land low and flat, a theme sustained by Môn, Anglesey, the island across the bay, and by the shore which will lead us, finally, to Afon Seiont and the very walls of Caernarfon.

Evening skies at Pontllyfni.
Peter Leslie

True, the blue-green mountains of Eryri continue to elevate the eastern horizon, but they neither command nor do they seek our attention. Our own prospect –island, bay and coast – is one of visual harmony and consolation: from the hazy, far-away prominence at Ynys Gybi, the white lighthouse of Llanddwyn, and the forest and sandy fringes around Newborough; to the gentle, level inflow at the mouth of Menai, Dinas

Evening skies at Pontllyfni.
Peter Leslie

hill, and, in the foreground, the mild bands and sweeps of muted colours, the ruffle of trees and scattering of stones.

Yet if the Peninsula has taught us anything, it must surely be that we should not presume to understand it. It is wily and volatile and may not be taken for granted. This apparently uneventful shore, for example, can become, in a few moments, the very eye of nature's anger. Within the meteorological compass of both the open sea and the feckless Rivals, its easy-going aspect can be swept aside with impertinent haste. See the sea darken out on the Irish horizon and in no time at all you can be overtaken by a storm: a blizzard of spindrift sleeting across the arc of the coast, high waves from nowhere, and plumes of spray swooshing over the beach lawn's gold-grey rocks and flicking the walls of the seaside villas.

Then, suddenly, out of the blue, an elemental truce! Swatches of clear sky, shafts of sunlight, a slackening wind, equable waters and a flamboyant rainbow. Before long, children playing on the sand drift beside the slipway, others struggling towards the water's edge with a red kayak; a man and dog heading for the river; sea anglers adjusting tripods and waiting for dusk.

Pontllyfni and beyond. The blue-green mountains of Eryri continue to elevate the eastern horizon.

David Clement

'Lord' David of Pontllyfni with Rupert.

The good life.

As evening approaches, the sky makes ready for a tremendous 'tropical' sunset. 'Palm trees' stand silhouetted against the crimson glow. Dolphins, returning to home waters, hurdle across the bay. The clink of sherry glasses and muted conversation drift from a beach lawn patio and mingle with waves of pensive music from the blue house. In the hollow, a chiminea crackles. Over the water, at the very edge of Ynys Gybi, South Stack lighthouse blinks steadily.

Perhaps, at low tide before sunset, you will glimpse the pillars of Arianrhod's citadel peeping from the shallow water. The Castle of the Silver Wheel, Caer Arianrhod, is one of these mystical places that haunt the shores of Penrhyn Llŷn; places where history and legend, fact and poetry merge. It was here, so tells *The Mabinogion*[28] that Queen Arianrhod, the virgin mother of Lleu, disowned her son and sent him away without weapons to defend himself. Help was at hand, however, in

Beach chalets, 1959.

David Clement

Looking west.

the person of Gwydion, the magician, who ensured that Lleu was protected from danger, while, by way of retribution, the wicked queen's castle was engulfed by the sea.

And there it lies today, a ruined citadel, an enchanted wheel of stones, or perhaps simply a natural semicircle of ancient weed-covered rocks.

It may come as some surprise to learn that here at Pontllyfni beach, we have left behind both the Heritage Coast and the Area of Outstanding Natural Beauty. For what, one might ask, could be more outstandingly and naturally beautiful than this? [29]

A feeling of infinity.

Above and below: Pontllfyni to Dinas. Oliver Hodgson

Guardians of the Straits at Fort Belan.

Michael Leeks

The Afon Llyfni, a short distance along the shore, is easy enough to ford at low tide, but at other times you may have to walk up to the main road, cross the bridge and return to the shore by following the river's northern bank. In a little over two miles of flat, stony beach walking, you will come to the motte at Dinas Dinlle – an Iron Age hill fort or an outpost of the Roman settlement of Segontium, whichever depiction pleases you more. Unfortunately, erosion has made the hill unsafe to climb.

A long frequently-lively, mostly-sandy beach stretches from Dinas Dinlle to Fort Belan, a handsome, practical, cannon-protected, never-to-have-been-aroused-in-anger fortress, which stands at the southern opening of the Menai Strait. The fortress – built by Thomas Wynn (whom we shall meet shortly) as a defence against French invasion – shares a small peninsula with the grandly-titled Caernarfon Airport, from where the adventurous may spread their wings over Penrhyn Llŷn, while the less intrepid visit the Air World Museum.

However, we shall do neither of these things. Instead, we shall turn to the east and walk along the lanes to the 'typically Welsh' village of Llandwrog.

Llandwrog village.

XVIII Lords and Ladies

Typically Welsh indeed! As a matter of fact, so little does Llandwrog resemble other villages in the area that, unless you have studied the runes of local history, its uniqueness might cause some confusion. A slender-spired church and cottages with protruding eaves and pointed arches create a certain Gothic flavour and make of the village something of a puzzle. Spiritually Welsh it certainly is, but its appearance is anything but *typically* so.

It is the church of St Twrog, however, tall and dominant, that contains the key to the village's mystery. Inside, a discreet chapel boasting an array of family monuments – not to mention a somewhat deferential atmosphere – indicates that this is a lordly shrine in a lordly village, and the lords (and ladies) in question are the Newboroughs.

In the chapel, screened from public scrutiny, family accolades abound: to the

The Harp.

Oliver Hodgson

cae'r
eglwys

Opposite and left:
A touch of Gothic.
Oliver Hodgson

first Lord Newborough (Sir Thomas Wynn), to William Percival Wynn, to Ellen, Sir John and Frances Wynn ('a bright example of piety and virtue'). Upright, masterful and celebrated Wynns; soldiers, botanists, county sheriffs, Members of Parliament, great and good, their merits hewn in stone.

One plaque in particular, however, simply demands closer inspection. It is a memorial, less imposing than the others, dedicated to

Rose Cottage. Cath Hope

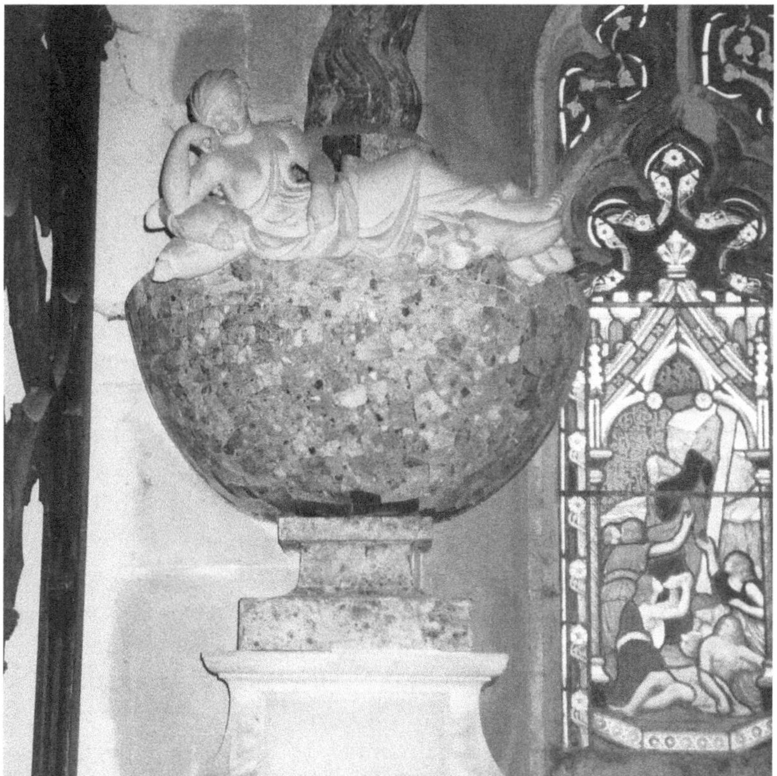

The Wynn Chapel.
Oliver Hodgson

The Maria Stella memorial.
Oliver Hodgson

a certain Maria Stella Petronilla, who died in Paris in 1843 and was buried in the cemetery at Montmartre on 31 December of that year.

Maria Stella Petronilla...the music of it!

But wait! We must attend to other matters before we recount Maria's remarkable story.

Traditional village centres are commonly occupied by two buildings of well-nigh equal importance, the church and the inn. Llandwrog is no exception to this.

Llandwrog's inn, the Harp (Ty'n Llan), is of ancient pedigree. A copy of a most venerable document hanging in her cosy bar illustrates some aspects of her own and of the area's history. Herewith, a selection of its disclosures:

Opposite: Inn and church, cheek to cheek.
Oliver Hodgson

The inn was 'used in the sixth century by Romans and pilgrims... a grave stone from the year AD680 points to the Roman occupation, as

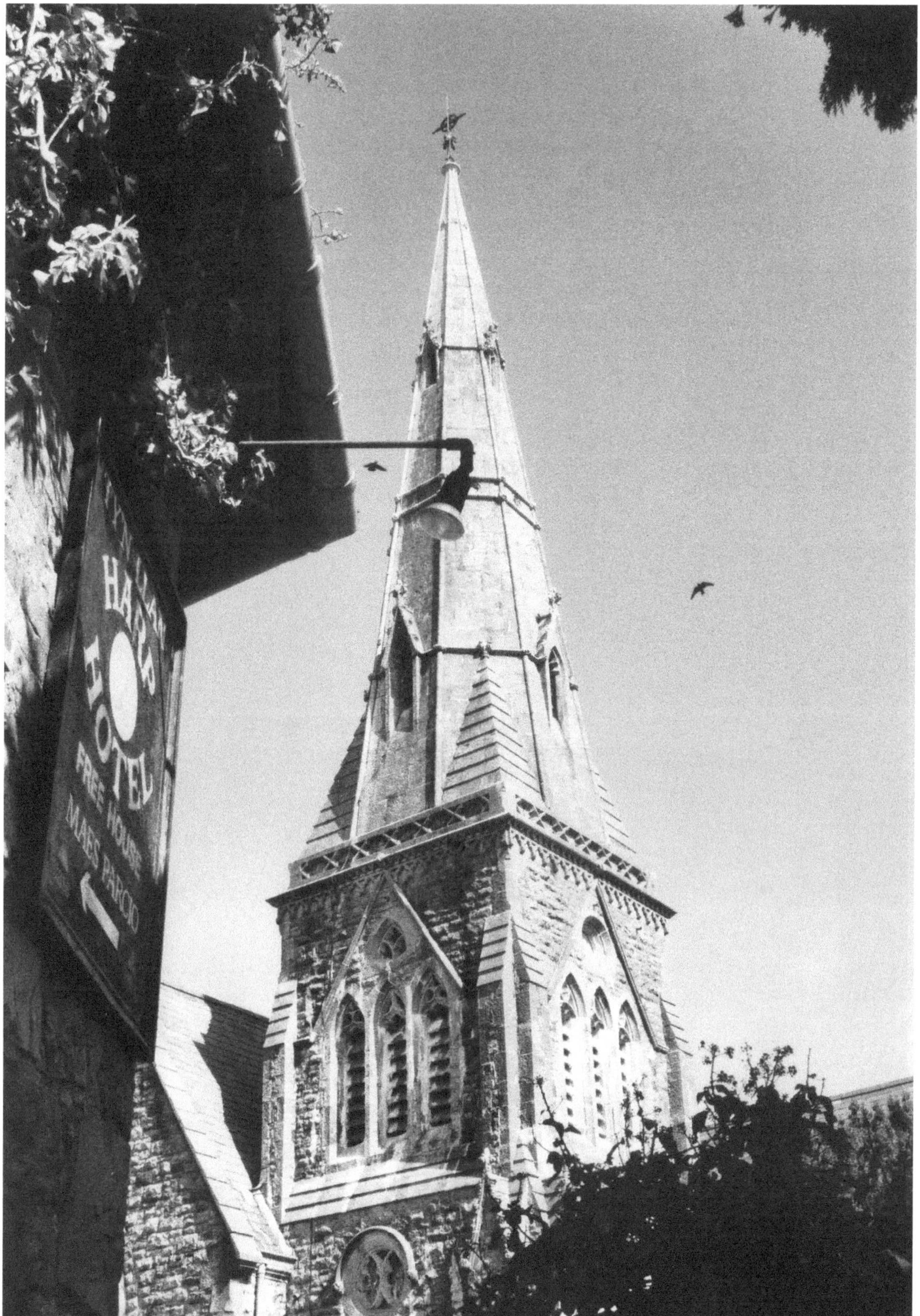
HARP
HOTEL
FREE HOUSE
MAES PARCIO

Opposite: The mansion, Glynllifon.

does Watling Street, beginning at Dinas Dinlle.' The document goes on to refer to 'a great plague in AD958 [which] decimated the people of Llantwrog,' and to Edgar, King of Britain, who, in AD961, demanded 300 wolves a year from Wales, including a substantial quota from Bodellog, Llanwnda, Llantwrog and Clynnog. From 1327 to 1377 the inn and the church formed part of the see of the Bishops of Bangor, and in 1790 a certain David Jones leased the building from the Rt Hon. Thos. Lord Newborough. In 1804 a license to 'Brew Ale' was granted to Thos. Jones Tygwyn. 'His inn was the farmhouse "Ty Ny Llan".' The inn was refurbished in 1856, 'at which time the church was entirely rebuilt by the Rt Hon. Spenser Bulkeley, Lord Newborough'.

Glynllifon

Half a mile to the south-east of Llandwrog, deeply wooded, firmly circumscribed by a seven-mile wall and secreted behind a 'triumphal' arch with lion and eagles, lies the estate and mansion of Glynllifon, the

Glynllifon's 'triumphal arch'.

The mansion's handsome façade.

former seat of the Wynn family and, accordingly, of the Lords and Ladies Newborough.

The Wynns, however, were by no means the first inhabitants of this charming woodland glade. Indeed not. For it is said that as early as the ninth century, a beautiful princess, Esyllt, and a handsome nobleman, Cilmyn Troed Ddu (Cilmyn Blackfoot), had married and settled here in a simple hut of mud and thatch.

With the passage of time, the family thus established became rich and influential. Politically shrewd, its members gained honours and inherited lands in recognition of their military deeds. They made wonderful gardens and built ever more substantial and opulent mansions. In the 17th century, Sir William Glyn – for so the family was called – created a house of unparalleled splendour, with windows of fine glass 'bright like Ebron's sun'.[30] He filled its chambers with hand-carved furnishings, decorated its walls with tapestries and set its tables with priceless silver.

The family name must have seemed imperishable, but it was not so. By the turn of the century the name was no more, for the lady Frances Glyn, who had inherited the estate, married Thomas Wynn of Boduan, a union of immense fortunes which would establish at Glynllifon a formidable new dynasty.

Former glories. The entrance hall at Glynllifon mansion.

The magnificent old stable block.

Maria Stella

We return now to the story of Maria Stella.

It is 1773, and in the Tuscan village of Modigliana, a daughter is born to the lowly Chiappini family. She is called Maria Stella Petronilla. Though she is held in affection by her father, Lorenzo, her mother, it is said, bears her malice. A certain Countess Camilla, however, a frequent visitor to the village, becomes fond of the child and often buys her presents and plays games with her.

When Maria is four, the family moves to Florence, Lorenzo having been employed by a company of Florentine noblemen. There they live in a fine villa, Maria is made to dress in expensive clothes, and is introduced to the skills and etiquette of the nobility. Much is required of her and she is often beaten by her mother for falling below the high expectations placed upon her. Such is her spirit, however, that she survives every ordeal. She becomes confident in society, and her musical prowess is the talk of the city.

One day, a middle-aged nobleman from across the sea comes to visit the Chiappinis. Impressed with the young girl's talents and roused by her beauty, he promptly informs her parents of his desire to marry her. Lorenzo is delighted (and, no doubt, handsomely compensated), but Maria is despondent. She is 13, the nobleman is 50.

The gentleman in question is none other than Thomas Wynn, Lord Newborough of Glynllifon. Notwithstanding Maria's reluctance, the union takes place, and in 1786 Maria Stella Petronilla Chiappini becomes the first Lady Newborough.

Six years later, Thomas Wynn returns to Wales with his young wife who dutifully and efficiently embraces her new regime. In 1802 and 1803 she gives birth to two sons – Thomas John and Spenser Bulkeley – and, though it had seemed unlikely at the time of her marriage, she enjoys an unprecedented degree of happiness.

In 1807, when Maria is 34, the First Lord passes away, and three years later, she meets and subsequently marries an Estonian nobleman. Together, they settle in Russia, but sadly the uncompromising terms of her first marriage deny her the company of her sons.

At which point Maria Stella might well have meekly subsided into the shadows of history. But no! Hers is a story never destined to have been of the 'happy ever after' kind. For now it takes a new turn, into the world of deathbed confessions, shifty politics, substituted babies and aristocratic jiggery pokery.

Lorenzo's dying words reveal that he is not, after all, Maria's father, but that she is in fact the daughter of a distinguished French nobleman, who, desperate for a male heir, had persuaded the Chiappinis to accept his baby girl in exchange for their newborn son. It would be a profitable transaction. They would receive both financial reward and social advancement, and an eminent lady would be appointed to watch over the baby girl.

True or false?

Let us for the moment assume truth. The French nobleman is no less a personage than the Duke of Orleans, Philippe Egalité. The son and heir he duly acquires from Lorenzo Chiappini will one day become Louis Philippe and will be crowned King of the French in 1830.

Think of these things, dear reader, as you pass beneath Glynllifon's triumphal arch. Think of the poetry of history! The Citizen King who may have been the son of a Tuscan peasant, and Maria Stella Petronilla, Lady Newborough, a princess of the Royal House of Orléans.[31]

Maria Stella.

We shift now to the middle of the 20th century. It is 1948 and, exhausted by the financial burden of repair and maintenance, the Fifth Lord Newborough, Thomas John Wynn, is forced to dispose of his beloved estate. Six years later, an Agricultural College opens on the site. The mansion, however, falls into disrepair, while the secret gardens and romantic woodland, neglected, become an impenetrable wilderness.

And now it is 1989. A date to celebrate! Gwynedd County Council unlocks the gates and declares open the Glynllifon Country Park. An extensive programme of restoration is undertaken. The public begin to trickle in.

And so to the present day. Notwithstanding the exuberance of its celebrated history, the park is best known as a site of special scientific importance, a dynamic centre for the contemporary arts and crafts, a lively venue for rallies, exhibitions and entertainments, and, not least, a place of lingering, timeless beauty.

Horseshoe bats and owls share tree-top shadows with birds of many a feather; badgers and otters tread and tumble below. Wild gardens and clear pools, park and pleasure ground, follies and forgotten figures revel in an unforeseen renaissance, and the trees of the exotic arboreta – from China, Japan and Algeria, not to mention the fantastic Giant American Redwoods – are indexed, labelled and proudly displayed.[32]

While time stands still in some of the old offices and workshops around the estate yard – ledgers, spectacles, paint pots and brushes locked in a perpetual past – in others, young craftspeople exercise their skills in iron, clay and glass. Artists gather in the timber mill gallery, and, in the engine house, Fred Dibnah's gleaming De Winton steam engine purrs smoothly into life.

True, much of the substance of the Newboroughs' history is becalmed in the shell of the Third Lord's empty mansion, which stands

Former estate workshops, now artists' studios.

– a little mournful perhaps – beyond the Afon Llifon, but the sorrow it may contain is amply retrieved by the children's boathouse, the hermitage and amphitheatre, and by the cascades, sculptures and fountains which illuminate every turning.

The engine house.

Opposite: Glynllifon.

The Black Cat Café.

And when you tire of this and that, try Mr Jefferies's Black Cat Café (Y Gath Ddu), its terrace buzzing with chatter, its kitchens ringing with laughter: Snowdonia Ploughman's Lunch with Black Bomber, Green Thunder and Red Devil; Artichoke Toast; Sarsparilla with Sparkling Welsh Water, all part and parcel of Mrs Griffiths's teasing menu.

Promenade: Llandwrog to Caernarfon

The lane that wanders from Llandwrog to Foryd Bay seems unaware of time and direction. Following the course of age-worn field boundaries and meandering streams, it strays first this way and then that, apparently quite indifferent to its fate. Accompanied by rolling meadows, lovely old 'manor house' farms and low stone bridges, the lane's lack of urgency captures the spirit of times quite different from our own. Yet, while we dawdle for a few moments in the past, less than

Foryd Bay.

a mile away busy main roads heave and conjure with matters of the present.

A little way beyond Blythe Farm before the white tower, the lane splits. Go straight on here, and soon you will come to a peaceful shore of tall reeds and mud banks and a shallow inter-tidal lagoon with golden plovers, widgeon, dunlins and curlews, where clouds of birds sometimes soar and swoop in unerring unison, and waders make elegant poses in the shallows. At low tide, see the sunlight making patterns of the delta-like tentacles that flow from two of the small rivers – Afon Carrog from the south, Afon Gwyrfai from the east – which drain into the bay.

Follow the lane as it curls inland towards Saron, cross the Gwyrfai via Pont Faen, and, after a short distance, return to the coast. Continuing north, you will see – taking form between Abermenai Point and Fort Belan – the Menai Strait, and you will recognise – since the Strait's powerful currents do not disturb the shallow lagoon – how it is that Foryd Bay is so calm.

We follow now – exactly – the line of the Strait, Ynys Môn to our left, wooded hills and bare fields to our right.

In such a field, standing like a tiny walled citadel, is the church of St Baglan, one of the oldest foundations in North Wales. Take the footpath from the lane and enter its quiet enclosure. See the Roman stones

Llanwnda Post Office, in the same family for more than 60 years.

Below and right: St Baglan's Church, friend of the friends of friendless churches. Oliver Hodgson

The ancient porch.
Cath Hope

embedded in its walls. Once close to decay, St Baglan's was saved from extinction by the Friends of Friendless Churches, in whose care it now rests.

We have now come very nearly to the end of our journey; behind us, 100 miles of footsteps. It is time, perhaps, to reflect. How will you best remember Penrhyn Llŷn? As a dramatic and beautiful place, strangely remote and untroubled by the conflicts of a modern world? As somewhere at the crossroads of history – a foot in each of the so-called 'two cultures' – pacing herself too cautiously for the reformer, too rashly for the traditionalist? Or perhaps you will recall a place on the edge of transition, eager to prosper, yet restrained by a determination to protect her Welshness – the gold dust of her history.

And since we speak of history once again, have you noticed how often the heroes and devils of the Llŷn tremble on the very brink of truth? How effortlessly they seem to slip in and out of myth? How frequently a sense of mystery permeates their stories, and how often they seem enhanced by the poetic tongue of their telling?

Notwithstanding veracity, that is exactly as history should be, 'a combination of magic, illusion, imagination, a whiff of what might have been, as elusive as woodsmoke on an October evening'.[33]

Little by little, as we come closer to the Afon Seiont, the fragments of

Caernarfon. Two thousand years of history awaits...
Oliver Hodgson

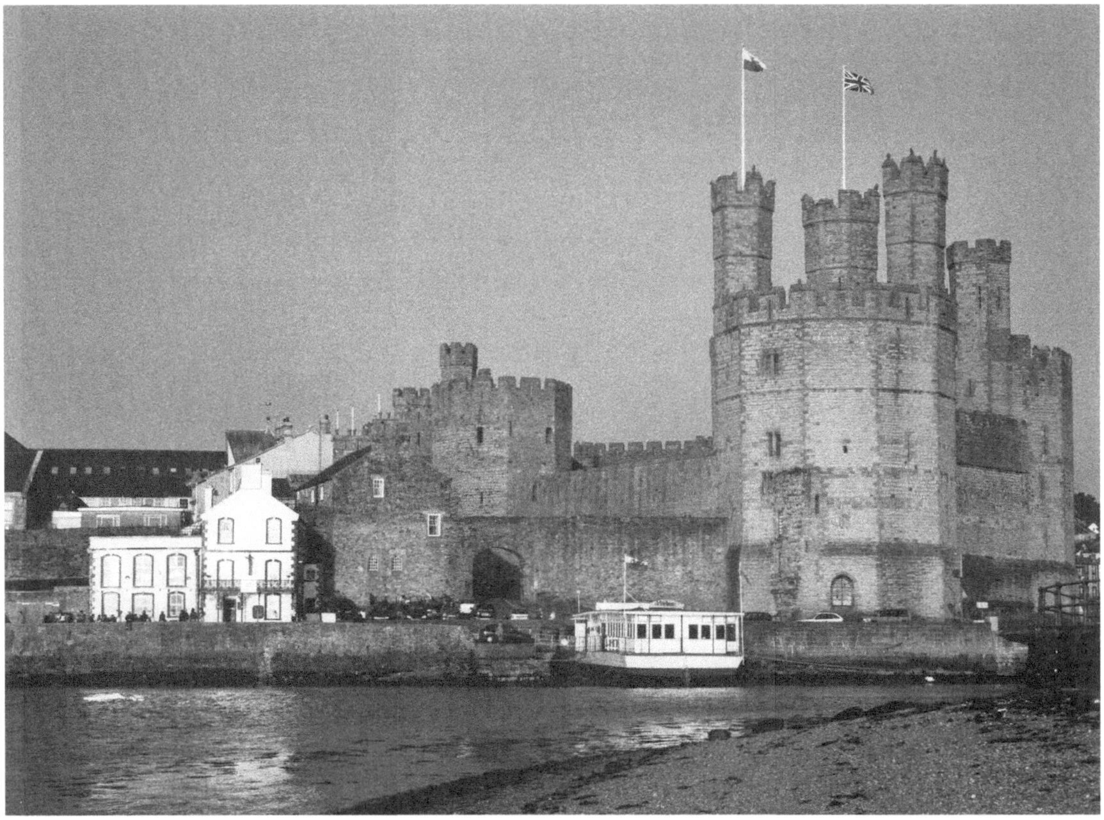

a town begin to creep across the nearby horizon. Turrets and spires, ships' masts, rugged quays, an inn – all drawn together by a massive sheltering wall. It is Caernarfon, port, market town, fortress. See how the Eagle tower – Tŵr Eryri – holds the bridge and commands the gate.

Across the river, 2,000 years of history awaits… Segontium, Constantium Ghaer-yn-Arfon. See the falcons and the ensigns, hear the drums, smell the powder.

Alas, dear reader! We must save Caernarfon for another day.

NOTES

1. Criccieth or Cricieth? That is the question: a question which embodies in a single letter, the frustrations of those who would strive to preserve the Welsh language. Since a double c is unknown in Welsh, I have chosen to use 'Cricieth' in *The Shores of Penrhyn Llŷn*.
2. Cymraeg is the first language of three-quarters of the population of the Llŷn.
3. Portmadoc had not, at that time, adopted its present spelling!
4. *Immortal Sails*, Henry Hughes, Stephenson, 1977.
5. *The Llŷn Coastal Path, Llwybr Arfordir Llŷn*, a free guide published by Gwynedd Council, will do much to enrich your journey.
6. See *Llŷn Pilgrims Trail, Teithiau'r Pererinion*, published by Gwynedd Council, for full details of the pilgrims' journeys.
7. *Wales. Epic Views of a Small Country*. Jan Morris, Penguin Books, 1986.
8. *Panorama from Castle Hill.* Hillaire Belloc.
9. *Criccieth – A Heritage Walk*, Eira and James Gleasure – a 'must' for the visitor!
10. *Travelling the World*, Paul Theroux, Penguin Books, 1992.
11. Cricieth Festival, David Lloyd George Memorial Lectures, sponsored by Dr W.R.P. George, CBE, and Mrs George. Supported by Gwynedd Council.
12. See *A Writer's House in Wales*, Jan Morris, National Geographic Directions, 2002.
13. There are at least two excellent street-by-street guides to Pwllheli: Dafydd Meirion's *A Walk Back in Time* and *Footpaths of Pwllheli*, by E. Griffith and E. Gruffydd.
14. Myrddin Fardd. Quoted by Elfed Gruffydd in *Llŷn* (Carreg Gwalch), 2003.
15. The Iron Man is at least the third figure to occupy this site. He was preceded by Mr Andrews's so-called *Canute*, and by Iron Man I – victim of climate and vandal.
16. *Llŷn*, Elfed Gruffydd, Carreg Gwalch, 2003. In the same paragraph (p138), Mr Gruffydd refers to an important related issue: that of increasing numbers of holidaymakers returning to the area as permanent residents, a trend serving 'to threaten the balance of the community'.
17. For many more facts and fables, treat yourself to *Welcome to Abersoch* by Ioan Roberts, Llygad Gwalch. It's concise and very entertaining!
18. It is not, in fact, impossible to continue along the shore from this point, but it is very difficult. Should you decide to do so, however,

do refer to Dafydd Meirion's no-nonsense guide, *Walking Llŷn's Shoreline*, Carreg Gwalch, 2005...and, pob lwc!

19. Though the coastal path is always under review, private farmland will occasionally force you inland. You would be wise, therefore, to use an up-to-date guide book and to follow directions assiduously.
20. Porth Dinllaen was acquired by the National Trust in 1944 through the Enterprise Neptune Appeal.
21. Quoted by Tom Morris. See below.
22. *Porthdinllaen, from Harbour to National Trust*, and *Morfa Nefyn a Phorthdinllaen, a Century of Change*, Tom Morris (Argraffwyd gan Wasg Carreg Gwalch).
23. *The Rough Guide to Wales*, Parker and Whitfield, Rough Guides, 2003.
24. Rupert Davies, 'Maigret,' is buried in the churchyard.
25. From *This Valley was Ours* by Eileen Webb, Gwasg, Carreg Gwalch, 1997. I am indebted to Mrs Webb for much of the material in this chapter.
26. Vortigern's Grave.
27. Nant Gwrtheyrn, Canolfan Iaith a Threftadaeth Cymru – the Welsh Language and Heritage Centre.
28. *The Mabinogion* is a collection of fantastic Celtic tales (translated by Gwyn Thomas and Thomas Jones, 1974).
29. At the time of writing there are signs of 'development' at Pontllyfni beach: luxurious holiday lodges, fitness centre, swimming pool and jet skis!
30. Quoted by Sian Lloyd Jones in *The Story of Glynllifon* (Gwynedd Council).
31. Maria Stella spends the last 22 years of her life in pursuit of evidence to support her royal claim. She becomes something of an embarrassment in France, and, in 1830, all copies of her memoirs are confiscated before they can be distributed.
32. CADW, the Welsh ancient monuments authority, has granted the gardens at Parc Glynllifon Grade I status.
33. Robert Lacey, author of *Great Tales from English History* (Little Brown).

Glossary of Place Names

A	
Aber	river mouth
Ardal	district
Afon	river
Allt	slope
B	
Bach	small
Bedd	grave
Betws	chapel
Bod	abode
Bryn	hill
Bwlch	pass
C	
Cae	field
Caer	fort
Capel	chapel
Carn	cairn
Carreg	crag/stone
Castell	castle
Cefn	ridge
Clogwyn	cliff
Clwyd	gate
Coch	red
Coed	wood
Cors	marsh/swamp
Craig	crag
Croes	cross
Cromlech	burial chamber
Cwm	valley
D	
Din	hillfort
Dinas	fort/city
Ddôl/Ddol	meadow
Du/Ddu	black
Dŵr	water
Dyffryn	valley
E	
Eglwys	church
Eryri	highland
F	
Fach	small
Faes	meadow
Fawr	large
Felin	mill
Fford	road
Ffynnon	well/spring
Foel	bare hill
G	
Gaer	camp
Galt	slope
Garn	eminence
Glan	riverbank
Glas	blue/green
Glyn	valley
Goch	red
Gors	swamp
Groes	cross
Gwyn	white
Gwynt	wind
H	
Hafod	summer dwelling
Hen	old
Hendre	winter dwelling
Heulog	sunny
Hir	long
I	
Is	below
Isaf	lower
L	
Llan	church
Llanerch	glade
Llech	stone
Llyn	lake
Llys	palace/court
Lôn	lane
M	
Maen	stone

Maes	field
Mawr	large
Melin	mill
Moel	bare hill
Môr	sea
Morfa	sea marsh
Mynydd	mountain
N	
Nant	stream
Newydd	new
O	
Ogof	cave
P	
Pandy	fulling mill
Pant	hollow
Parc	park
Pen	point/head
Penryhn	promontory
Pentir	headland
Pentref	village
Pistyll	waterfall
Plas	mansion
Pont	bridge
Porth	port
Pwll	pool
R	
Rhaeadr	waterfall
Rhiw	hill
Rhos	moor
Rhyd	ford
S	
Sarn	causeway
Sir	shire
T	
Tafarn	inn
Traeth	beach
Tref	town
Trwyn	promontory
Tŵr	tower
Tŷ	house
Tyddyn	small holding
Ty'n Llan	village
U	
Uchaf	upper
W	
Waun	moorland
Wen	white
Wern	alder swamp
Y	
Y, Yr	the
Yn	in
Ynys	island

References

Avent, R. *Criccieth Castle, Pennarth Fawr* CADW, 1989.

Banholzer, K.F. *Old Carnarvon – Outside the Town Walls* 1998.

Beazley, E. *A Taste of Madocks* P & Q, 1994.

Beazley, E. *Madocks and the Wonder of Wales* Faber & Faber, 1967.

Bevan, R.M. *Pwllheli* R.M. Bevan, 1980.

Burras N. and J. Stiff *Walks on the Llŷn Peninsula, Part I, South and West* Gwasg Carreg Gwalch, 1995.

Burras N. and J. Stiff *Walks on the Llŷn Peninsula, Part II, North and East* Gwasg Carreg Gwalch, 1996.

Cantrell, J. *The Lleyn Peninsula Coastal Path* Cicerone,1997.

Du Parcq, H. *Life of David Lloyd George* (Vol I) Caxton, 1912.

Eames, Aled *Shrouded Quays* Carreg Gwalch, 1991.

Eames, Aled *Ships and Seamen of Gwynedd* Gwynedd Archives, 1976.

Gleasure, E. and J. *Criccieth: A Heritage Walk* Eifionydd History Society, 1998.

Griffith E. and E. Gruffydd *Footpaths of Pwllheli* Gwasg Carreg Gwalch.

Gruffydd, E. *Llŷn* Gwasg Carreg Gwalch, 2004.

Harris, Jan *Walking the Lleyn Coast* Walking Routes, Clywd, 1995.

Hole A., E. O'Carroll and J. King *Wales* Lonely Planet, 2004.

Hughes J.H. and G.E. Thomas *Glynllifon* Education Office, Caernarfon, 1972.

Hughes, H. *Immortal Sails* Stephenson.

Jones, Sian Lloyd *The Story of Glynllifon* Gwynedd Council, 2006.

Lacey, Robert *Great Tales from English History* Little, Brown.

Lloyd Hughes, D.G. *Pwllheli: An Old Welsh Town and its History* Gwasg Gomr, 1994.

Meirion, D. *Walking Llŷn's Shoreline* Gwasg Carreg Gwalch, 2004.

Meirion, D. *A Walk Back in Time, Pwllheli* Llais Publications, 2005.

Morris, Jan *Wales, Epic Views of a Small Country* Penguin, 1986.

Morris, Jan *A Writer's House in Wales* National Geographic Society, 2002.

Morris, Jan *Coronation Everest* Faber & Faber, 1958.

Morris, Myfanwy *Porthmadog* Gwynedd Archives and Museum Service.

Morris, T. *Porthdinllaen, from Harbour to National Trust* Wasg Carreg Gwalch.

Morris, T. *Morfa Nefyn a Phorthdinllaen, A Century of Change* Wasg Carreg Gwalch.

Mowat, C.L. *Lloyd George* Oxford University Press, 1964.

Parker M. and P. Whitfield *The Rough Guide to Wales* Rough Guides, 2000.

Perrott, D. *Walking Round Porthmadog* Kittiwake, 2002.
Roberts, I. *Welcome to Abersoch/Llanbedrog* Llygad Gwalch.
Roberts, I. *Welcome to Pwllheli* Llygad Gwalch.
Roberts, Tony *See the Lleyn Peninsula* Abercastle Publications, 1992.
Rogers, C. *Walking on the Lleyn Peninsula* Mara Publications, 1999.
Senior, Michael *Figures in a Landscape Part 2* Carreg Gwalch, 2000.
Theroux, P. *Travelling the World* Penguin, 1992.
Thomas R. and P. Kay *Llŷn, A Special Place* The National Trust, 1998.
Thomas R. *Walks on Llŷn. Porthor, Carreg & Mynydd Anelog* The National Trust.
Titchmarsh *Exploring Snowdonia, Anglesey and the Lleyn Peninsula* Jarrold.
Webb, E.M. *This Valley was Ours* Gwasg Carreg Gwalch, 1997.
Williams, W.A. *Old Pwllheli* Vols I & II Bridge Books, 1991 & 1992.

Other Sources

Plas yn Rhiw Honora Keating.
Llŷn Coastal Path Gwynedd Council.
Llŷn Peninsula, Area of Outstanding Natural Beauty Countryside Council for Wales.
Llŷn Pilgrims Trail Gwynedd Council.
St Hywyn's Church, Our Maritime Heritage Archives of the Ship Hotel, Aberdaron.
An Introduction to Porthmadog Harbour Gwynedd Archives Dept.
Tremadog, Historic Planned Town Cyfeillion Cadw Tremadog, 1995.
*Porthmadog, Tremadog, Borth-y-Ges*t The Porthmadog Chamber of Trades and Commerce and Porthmadog Town Council.
Lloyd George Museum Gwynedd Culture and Leisure.
CADW Welsh Historic Monuments, What is Listing?
Abersoch Sensation Magazine Zoe McLennon (ed.)
North Wales Illustrated Guide NW Holiday Resorts Association.

Various leisure and events guides, maps and publicity leaflets and, by no means least, the *Daily Post*, the *Cambrian News* and the *Caernarfon and Denbigh Herald.*

* 9 7 8 1 7 8 0 9 1 4 4 3 5 *

ND - #0234 - 270225 - C0 - 260/195/8 - PB - 9781780914435 - Gloss Lamination